INNOVATE THE
PIXAR WAY

BUSINESS LESSONS FROM THE WORLD'S MOST CREATIVE CORPORATE PLAYGROUND

BILL CAPODAGLI AND LYNN JACKSON
bestselling authors of *The Disney Way*

New York   Chicago   San Francisco   Lisbon   London   Madrid   Mexico City
Milan   New Delhi   San Juan   Seoul   Singapore   Sydney   Toronto

Library of Congress Cataloging-in-Publication Data

Capodagli, Bill, 1948.
   Innovate the Pixar Way : business lessons from the world's most
creative corporate playground / by Bill Capodagli and Lynn Jackson.
      p.   cm.
   ISBN 978-0-07-163893-7
   1. Pixar (Firm) — Management.   2. Creative ability in
business.   3. Organizational change.   4. Technological innovations —
Management.

HD53 .C369   2009
658.4'063—dc22   2009029691

1 2 3 4 5 6 7 8 9 10 11 12 13 14 15 16 17 18 19 20   WFR/WFR   0 9

ISBN   978-0-07-163893-7
MHID   0-07-163893-8

Illustrations by Googenius

We dedicate this book to the memory of

Walt Disney....

He inspired us to dream, believe, dare, and do.

Contents

Acknowledgments   vii
Introduction: Why Pixar?   ix
About the Authors   xiii

1   Remember the Magic of Childhood   1
2   Where Did the Creativity Go?   7
3   Hey, Kids, Let's Put on a Show!   13

SECTION 1   DREAM LIKE A CHILD

4   Dream for Infinity and Beyond:
    The Beginnings of Pixar   25
5   A New Way to Play "Follow the Leader"   37

SECTION 2   BELIEVE IN YOUR PLAYMATES

6   Collaboration in the Sandbox   51
7   Stand Together Against the Bullies   67

SECTION 3 DARE TO JUMP IN THE WATER AND
           MAKE WAVES

      8 The Skater Who Never Falls
         Will Never Win the Gold!   75
      9 Recess: Go Out and Play!   83
     10 Forty-One Neat Things to
         Unleash Your Imagination   97

SECTION 4 DO UNLEASH YOUR
           CHILDLIKE POTENTIAL

     11 How Do You Measure a Dream?   115
     12 "Let's Make a Dent in the Universe"   125
     13 Ready, Set, Go!   135

Appendix A Other Corporate Playgrounds   151
Appendix B Bill and Lynn's Favorite Fun Facts
            About Pixar   175
Appendix C Through a Child's Eyes   181
            References   193
            Index   203

Acknowledgments

WE WISH TO thank our fabulously innovative and insightful McGraw-Hill editorial director, Mary Glenn, who believed that there is much to learn from Pixar about how to establish and manage an exciting corporate playground! Her support of more than ten years means so much to us!

A huge thank-you to Alvy Ray Smith, cofounder of Pixar, who set us straight on many of the facts regarding Pixar's beginnings. He is a totally authentic guy who is also a lot of fun!

Big kudos to our "corporate playground" people at Google, Griffin Hospital, Men's Wearhouse, Nike, Target, and Zappos for their cooperation and cool insights.

And a heartfelt thank-you to our manuscript editor, Joan Hoffman, who is one of the best researchers and critical evaluators on the planet! She continues to challenge us on our writing projects.

A special thanks to our graphic designer and creative consultant, Wade Gugino, whose creativity amazes us. A heartfelt thanks to our friends and creative consultants, Lorma (executive director of the Holland Area Arts Council) and Ken Freestone (project manager, West Michigan Strategic Alliance), who have a wonderful command of the creative process and who continue to inspire those of us in west Michigan!

We are grateful to the Tucson Unified School District Opening Minds Through the Arts (OMA) champions and students for their inspiration. A special thank you to Joan Ashcraft, Donn Poll, Rick Wamer, and OMA's national spokesperson, Broadway legend Carol Lawrence.

Finally, we are grateful to Ken Blanchard, Stephen Covey, George Zimmer, Brian Walker, and John Christensen for their continued support of our work.

Introduction

Why Pixar?

ASK ALMOST ANY child you know to tell you about Buzz Lightyear, Nemo, or Lightning McQueen, and you will believe that you are hearing a story about a trusted friend. These beloved animated characters were born in a child-like storytelling "playground" known as Pixar—a place that enables storytellers to create tales of friends and foes who share great adventures in enchanting lands. Their heartfelt stories will continue to be passed on, from child to adult, from adult to child, for generations to come.

Doc Hudson, town judge and doctor in the 2006 cinematic blockbuster *Cars,* could have been describing the Pixar culture as clearly as he was describing the town atmosphere of Radiator Springs when he said: "These are good folk around here who care about one another. I don't want them depending on someone they can't count on."

And, at Pixar, Ed Catmull leads a team of innovators who truly count on one another.

As cofounder of Pixar and current president of Pixar and Disney Animation Studios, Catmull's leadership role model is Walt Disney himself—the man who reinvented the entire animation business. Like Walt, Ed reinvented animated feature film technology, set a new standard for storytelling, and masterfully established an innovative corporate culture. Collective creativity within a corporate culture never happens by accident. It begins with creative leadership that is trustworthy and in turn trusts others to accomplish big dreams. And, in the case of Pixar, the preponderance of evidence attesting to their success is unquestionable, from producing the first fully computer-generated feature film (*Toy Story*, 1995) to churning out one box-office hit after another and amassing numerous industry awards.

In stark contrast to the crippling short-term mentality that has become a cancer in American business culture today, the Pixar organization honors the legacy of Walt Disney by refusing to take shortcuts, by fulfilling the promise of bringing the story to life in each and every movie they make, and by championing a simple formula espoused by the stratospherically gifted chief creative officer of Pixar and Disney Animation Studios, John Lasseter: "Quality is the best business plan of all."

In 1984, Pixar cofounders Ed Catmull and Alvy Ray Smith, while leading the computer graphics division at Lucasfilm, made the best hire of their lives when they landed John Lasseter. (In 1986, Steve Jobs purchased Pixar from Lucasfilm. Alvy would leave the organization in 1991 to pursue other dreams.) Lasseter's personal credo—heart, inventiveness, and inspiration—is imbedded deep in the creation of each Pixar film and may be the true key to Pixar's ability to continue to produce great stories with mass appeal.

Since 2006, when The Walt Disney Company purchased Pixar from then-owner Steve Jobs for $7.4 billion in stock, Ed and John have been energizing Disney with their innovative genius. At the time, Ed said, "Disney has had two major heydays [referring to the 1930s, when Walt Disney pioneered the animated feature-film art form, and the 1980s, when the animation renaissance was made possible by a new leadership team], and we're going to make a third." And although they are realizing that dream, John Lasseter believes, "Success doesn't just breed success—it breeds autonomy, which in turn nurtures creativity."

For twenty-five years, Catmull and Lasseter have worked side by side in a collegiate manner that is reminiscent of the partnership between Walt Disney and his brother Roy, who founded their movie studio in 1923. We believe their greatest shared attribute is the ability to view the world through the eyes of a child. As Lasseter explained, "People who get into animation tend to be kids. We don't have to grow up. But, also, animators are great observers, and there's this childlike wonder and interest in the world—the observation of little things that happen in life."

Childlike dreamers, producers of "good show," champions of artists, protectors of an innovative culture—these are the hallmarks of three legendary filmmakers: Walt Disney, Ed Catmull, and John Lasseter.

Indeed, Pixar is a "playground" that will inspire you to:

Dream *like a child.*
Believe *in your playmates.*
Dare *to jump in the water and make waves.*
Do *unleash your childlike potential.*

About the Authors

RATHER THAN WRITE about our collective half century of consulting and training experience with both entrepreneurial and Fortune 500 companies (you can read about us on our website: www.capojac.com), we thought we'd share our answers to a questionnaire inspired by the one James Lipton uses in the Bravo television program "Inside the Actors Studio":

1. What do you have in common with Ed Catmull?
   Bill and Lynn:
      An idol: Walt Disney
      American Idol fans

2. What do you have in common with John Lasseter?
   Bill and Lynn:
      An idol: Walt Disney
      A love of good wine (John owns The Lasseter
      Family Winery in Sonoma. Unfortunately, they
      can't send his wine to our great state of Michi-
      gan . . . yet!)

3. What is your favorite Pixar character?
   Bill: Doc from *Cars*
   Lynn: Sally from *Cars*

4. What is your favorite Pixar curse word?
      Oops! These never make it into a picture. They
      only happen on the "closed set."

5. What Pixar movie turns you on?
   Bill: *Toy Story;* this is where it all started.
   Lynn: *Finding Nemo;* I love the ocean.

6. What is your favorite Pixar movie line?
   Bill: "These are good folk around here who care
      about one another. I don't want them depend-
      ing on someone they can't count on." —Doc
      from *Cars*
   Lynn: "Hey there, Mr. Grumpy Gills. When life
      gets you down do you wanna know what you've
      gotta do? Just keep swimming." —Dori from
      Finding Nemo

7. What Pixar character would you *not* want to be?
    Bill: Nemo's mother; she gets eaten in the first
    scene.
    Lynn: Bo Peep; she has to stay home when the
    boys get to go out and find Woody.

8. What is your favorite Pixar song?
    Bill: "You've Got a Friend in Me" from *Toy Story*
    Lynn: "Beyond the Sea" from *Finding Nemo*

9. What do you like best about Pixar?
    Bill: their collegiate and "childlike" culture
    Lynn: Bob Iger (president and CEO of The Walt
    Disney Company), who allows Pixar to main-
    tain their freedom

10. If heaven exists, what would you like God to say to you
    when you arrive at the Pearly Gates?
    Bill and Lynn:
        "You have cleared the wait list and are just in time
        to join Walt Disney for the premiere of his new
        stellar 4-D animated feature film!"

1

Remember the Magic of Childhood

WHEN WE BEGAN writing this book, our goal was to unveil the secrets of Pixar's innovative genius. Our first thought was to, as Lieutenant Casselle said in *Casablanca,* "Round up the usual suspects"—leadership, teaming, training, culture. As we investigated each one, we found that indeed, all of these "usual suspects" *do* contribute to Pixar's success. But which of these, if any, was the essence, the source, the head waters, the "big bang" of Pixar's creativity?

After perusing our library of Pixar films, it dawned on us—of course—*Toy Story* held the answer: looking at the world through the eyes of a child or a child's toys. This is how Pixar continues to catch lightning in a bottle. Pixar director Pete Docter (*Monsters, Inc., Up*) revealed, "As naïve as it may sound, making *Toy Story* felt like an extension of school, where we were just making the film we wanted to make for us and our friends to enjoy."

When we were children the truth lived in our imaginations—where we were the princesses in the castle or the knights in shining armor slaying the dragon. In our minds, we could do anything! But then parents, teachers, and bosses chased the little kid right out of us. Dreaming, making believe, acting impulsively, and taking risks were not rewarded in the "real world"—the adult world. We must follow the rules. The small child became silent, but childhood dreams are resilient and remain hidden away in the deepest caverns of our minds. In the Pixar "playground," employees are free to let loose their childlike "magic" and energy.

Recently, Bill witnessed firsthand how the Tucson Unified School District is reinventing the learning experience and capitalizing on that childlike dreaming through its Opening Minds Through the Arts (OMA) program. The George Lucas Educational Foundation features OMA as one of the few shining examples of a uniquely creative K–12 learning environment (see edutopia.org/arts-opening-minds-integration). OMA's vision of "improving student achievement by building connections between the arts and the curriculum" is akin to Pixar's mantra "Art is a team sport." During the first half of the school year in OMA, first graders learn about opera and the value of the collaborative process. During the second half of the school year, students write their own operas, and these formal artistic learning experiences continue through the fifth grade. Instead of stifling their imaginations, OMA is opening new worlds to these children by allowing them to dream. As Donn Poll, executive director of the OMA Foundation, remarked, "With the use of arts integration comes the enormous opportunity to bring *every child* the opportunity to love the process of learning, and to be engaged on the level of their own passion—this carries forth throughout their lives in anything else they want to learn."

"OMA means Opening Minds through the Arts, so I open my mind and draw everything. I can let my imagination take me anywhere I want."

—Juwan, OMA grade school student

Any "kid" who is lucky enough to "carry forth" into the world of Pixar finds a company who lives its credo: dream like a child. Pixar is a unique blend of both technically and artistically creative people who are continually engaged in their passions for making movies. And certainly, the childlike atmosphere in Pixar's Emeryville, California, "playground" sparks its employees' collective creativity on a level that has become the envy of employees in countless other organizations. In the words of Alvy Ray Smith, "When I sit around and watch the animators, it seems that they have managed to hold onto childhood. They surround themselves with toys, and they just have a lot of fun like kids. That's one of the reasons they are so damn much fun to be around—they're sort of constantly fun, playful, setting up little secret rooms—you just don't know what they are going to do next."

Unfortunately, however, most organizations have no interest in and no knowledge of what it takes to produce such an energizing environment. It begins with creating a culture where imagination—the very thing that kept us so interested in discovering and trying new things when we were young—is cherished and rewarded. So, who better than kids themselves to help remind us that we need to remove the haze from our childhood eyes of wonder? When it comes to unleashing creativity, the *little* children of OMA have some *big* messages to share, and we have included them in Appendix C, "Through a Child's Eyes."

Don't let life beat the kid out of you. . . .

It is never too late to remember the magic!

Bill and Lynn's Chalkboard

Remember: childhood
is not an age but rather
a state of mind.

2

Where Did the Creativity Go?

DID YOU EVER wonder why it took so long for the fast-food hamburger business, started by White Castle back in 1912, to become such a staple of the American way of life? It took a creative visionary like Ray Kroc, who was influenced by another visionary—Henry Ford and his assembly line production innovations. In 1961, Kroc bought McDonald's from the McDonald brothers, and the rest is history. Likewise, the discount department store has been around for more than a century—Woolworth dime stores date back to 1879, followed by Kresge's in 1899 and Ben Franklin Stores in 1927. Again, it took a creative visionary—this time Sam Walton—to open Wal-Mart Discount City in Rodgers, Arkansas, in 1962 to forever change the discount retail market. When Walt Disney arrived in Hollywood in 1923 to begin his animated cartoon business, he thought he came too late to really make a name for himself. By that time, Felix the Cat, a creation of the Pat Sullivan Studios, had already attained superstar status. But instead of giving up, Walt reinvented animation. Rather than using the slap-stick gags so popular at the time, he created characters with unique personalities that have endured for decades— Mickey Mouse, Minnie Mouse, Goofy, Donald Duck, the list goes on and on. These characters continue to capture the hearts of children today, and Mickey has been around for more than eighty years!

What does all this mean? Clearly, the first to market, while initially being creative, can lose focus and fade into relative obscurity over time. Slowly, that imagination that once soared on wings like Buzz Lightyear finally crashes into the ground. (Buzz's wings didn't make him fly; he only thought they could.) Why is it that only once in a while an organization totally redefines its industry? Why can't every organization be innovative? There's the typical lineup of excuses—"We tried that before"; "That's too crazy to consider"; "There's nothing wrong with what we're doing"; "That's not my job"—and so on and so on. The worst excuse of all is when managers say, "We aren't an innovative organization." Too many shortsightedly reserve the label "innovator" for the "big-league" brands like Apple,

Nike, or Google, who are associated with recognizable, simple, and sexy products. Therefore, they just don't view themselves as very creative.

Consider the creative talents of the following two groups who were asked these three questions: How many of you are good singers; how many of you are good dancers; and how many of you are good artists? About 2 percent of the first group responded positively to each of these three questions. This response is typical of most business teams with whom we've worked. We tell teams that it would be easy to find a second group in any community who would give nearly 100 percent positive responses. Surprised? Ask just about any group of first graders these three questions, and the children will respond with an enthusiastic "Yes!" to each one. All children are creative—they're born that way!

What happened to the creative gene that was so alive in our childhoods? J. M. Barrie, author of *Peter Pan*, once said, "Nothing that happens after we are twelve matters very much." Maybe twelve is the age that we stop believing in the power of dreams—when we stop taking risks and pursuing big ideas. Maybe twelve is the age we become practical and in touch with "reality." As a self-confessed Peter Pan, John Lasseter is used to trying out new things, and he doesn't fear results that are different from what he expected them to be. John has said, "At Pixar we're almost more excited about the things that didn't work because it's like: well, we tried this, but we didn't expect this. It's like a trapeze artist who's going to do a quintuple somersault—it's never been done before in the world. Hollywood is a place where, typically, if something doesn't work you lose your job. In Hollywood terms, not only is there no net but there's poison spikes down there. Whereas at Pixar we don't just have a net, we have down comforters and air bags, and you have everybody trying stuff constantly. That's one of the things we've changed here." Pixar continuously strives to forge new frontiers and is one of the premiere business models of innovative cultures in America, and perhaps the entire world.

For more than a hundred years, American business has been conditioned by leading management experts, beginning in the late 1890s with Frederick W. Taylor's teachings on scientific industrial efficiency; Henry Ford's 1913 assembly line process for building things faster and cheaper; and Dr. Deming's 1950s quality management lessons emphasizing how to remove variation from the manufacturing process. The message over the years has been consistent: reduce cost and remove variation.

Today we expect companies to be disciplined, but we also ask them to be innovative, which by its very nature increases cost and variation. Once the newest iPod, flat-screen TV, or laptop is developed, the push for creativity and innovation gets ignored and focus returns to reducing costs. Innovation can be costly; the trick is to be innovative *and* profitable. But priorities are constantly changing, and organizations must adapt on a continuous basis. Most find it difficult if not impossible to emphasize creativity and innovation while controlling costs for the long term.

So, how do you build an organization that embraces change and delivers an innovative, fairly priced, high-quality, and profitable product? How do you establish a culture of creativity in which the talents and abilities of all are nurtured and honed with great care? How do you unleash the creative genius within your employees and still meet budgets and deadlines? How do you establish an environment that awakens dreams?

Very few organizations today maintain the balance between childlike dreamer and task-driven doer. When it comes to innovation, like Walt Disney, Pixar is an industry pacesetter. In this book, we reveal how Pixar has reawakened the innovative spirit of Walt Disney. You will not only learn how leaders Ed Catmull and John Lasseter have given birth to a unique culture that is both innovative and profitable but also how you can create your own innovative playground.

Lucky for us, Walt Disney, Ed Catmull, and John Lasseter never lost that childlike innocence. They knew how to Dream, Believe, Dare, Do. But first, one word of caution: "Innovate, don't imitate!" You need to define a culture that is uniquely yours, one that is right for your organization— it takes time and hard work to make it happen.

There's no instant pudding!

Bill and Lynn's Chalkboard

Through our consulting experience,
we have discovered that creativity
abounds in all organizations...
you simply have to unleash it!

3

Hey, Kids,
Let's Put on a Show!

KENNY ORTEGA, CREATOR of the Disney blockbuster *High School Musical* craze, said that the source of his inspiration was the old Judy Garland and Mickey Rooney musicals of the 1930s and 1940s. Two lessons can be learned from these musicals. The first is to think like a director, and the second is to avoid overexposure—don't overdo a good thing.

Let's start with lesson number two—avoiding overexposure. In the late 1990s, Disney began to produce films that critics called "formulaic," much like the Garland-Rooney string of "Hey, kids, let's put on a show!" variations—*Strike Up the Band* (1940), *Babes on Broadway* (1940), and *Girl Crazy* (1943). Disney's string began with *The Second Jungle Book: Mowgli and Baloo* (1997) and *The Lion King II* (1998), followed by *102 Dalmatians* (2000)—the list continues with another eleven rather unimaginative productions.

Walt Disney himself refused to do feature film sequels. He didn't want to waste the money and creative talent on old ideas. He wanted to use his resources to create, not to simply copy a successful past production. Pixar president Ed Catmull said, "When Walt Disney was alive, he continually changed and adapted. Nothing ever stayed the same. And when he died, that's when things froze. And people were saying, 'What would Walt do?' But, when he was alive . . . he kept doing things. [At Pixar] . . . we are continuing that heritage of changing as technology changes. . . . We will continue to do things that are new and different." Pixar University dean Randy Nelson remarked, "Everyone here loves the old Disney films, but we never want to do those movies where the audience can figure out there must be a song coming here or 'He's an orphan, so he's going to have a fat little buddy.'" As Andrew Slabin, a Merrill Lynch entertainment analyst, said, "What makes a movie successful is not only the technology but the story that brings people to see it over and over—it's got to be heartfelt and warm. That's what Pixar movies do." Pixar's only sequel to date has been *Toy Story 2* (1999), which was before the Pixar acquisition by Disney. Disney had been distributing and cofinancing their films and encouraged Pixar to make *Toy Story 2* as a lower cost and quality "direct to video" film. John Lasseter commented, "These were the people that put out *Cinderella II*. We believe that the only reason to do a sequel is if you have a great story, period. . . . We want these [Pixar] films to be at the same level of the films Walt Disney made. I mean, look, he made *Snow White and the Seven Dwarfs*, *Pinocchio*, *Fantasia*, *Dumbo*, *Bambi*, and *Peter Pan*. Those films . . . will always live forever." *Toy Story 2* went on to have a new story of its own, premier in theaters, and become a critical and commercial success, solidifying Pixar's obsession that there should be only one quality measurement for every film: it begins and ends around the *story*. (As this book goes to print, *Toy Story 3* and *Cars 2* are in production—and we believe that the story will still "be king!")

So, don't just copy your old and boring product or service—destroy, demolish, eradicate, nuke, vaporize, and zap it! Once you have totally wiped out the old, you can apply the first lesson from our musical history examples—to think like a director. Think of your team or business as if you were the director of a Broadway play. Sit in the director's chair and visualize the major pieces of the production and direction of the play—the story, setting, roles, and backstage processes.

Begin with the Story

What's your dream? What are the customers' dreams? What story are you trying to tell? What mood are you setting? How do you want your customers to feel after their experience with your organization?

Redefine Your Product or Service

Walt Disney World is not just a theme park or resort. It is an *experience* that allows us to leave the real world far behind us and become Peter Pan or Cinderella—a three-dimensional fantasy taking place before our very eyes, a larger-than-life experience. Lasseter, who is now spending half of his time advising Disney on how to keep the "magic" alive in its theme parks, said, "The hardest thing to get is true emotion. I always believe you need to earn that with the audience. You can't just tell them, 'OK, be sad now.' . . . Even to the last minute you can be adding little bits of humor. But the true earned emotion is something that you really have to craft." It doesn't matter if you are creating the next Pixar animated feature film, designing a new refrigerator, opening a new restaurant, or reengineering your accounts receivable process, you have to bring your vision, your story, your dream to life in an exciting and exhilarating way. As Ed Catmull explained, "Our directors have to be masters at knowing how to tell a story. This means they must have a unified vision, one that will give coherence to the thousands of ideas that go into a movie." Not only does the story have to be engaging for the team but it must also make an emotional connection with the customer. And at Pixar, "story is king"—everything that goes into the development of a Pixar film is in support of telling the best story they can.

Get into the Dream-Fulfillment Business

Craft your story in a way that will ignite the creative energies of your team and make magical, dream-come-true moments for your customers.

Instead of "meeting customer expectations," start fulfilling their dreams. Craft the customer experience in terms of:

- Three-dimensional Technicolor images
  - Dreams fulfilled
  - Magical moments
  - Doing the impossible
  - Story, plot, theme
  - Unique, memorable, and engaging
  - Passionate belief in values

Build the Set

If you were a director of a Broadway play, you would have a set designer whose job it is to make sure the visual journey of the audience complements the overall story. Like Walt Disney, John Lasseter is fanatical about details—"Every detail has to be thought out, designed, modeled, shaded, placed, and lit. . . . It takes four years to make one of these films and there are no excuses after the movie's done. It's going to be that way forever. . . . Just try to think of another film from 1938 that is watched as much today as *Snow White* is, or even go to 1995 and *Toy Story*."

What should your set look like? If you are designing a new software program, how do colors, packaging, and documentation contribute to the overall customer experience? Early in the development of Intuit's personal accounting software program Quicken, Intuit engineers traveled all around the country to observe and interview customers who had purchased their product. They even arranged for in-home customer visits to observe and record the ease of installation, from opening the package to understanding the instructions to using the program for paying bills and creating household budgets.

The "virtual set" in today's electronic environment is immense and includes everything from the parking lot, store front, and product display to the website, business cards, phone systems, and warehouses. As Lasseter confirmed, every detail needs to be "thought out, designed, modeled, shaded, and lit." The setting is part of the creative experience—don't overlook or shortchange it.

Recruit the Cast

As the director of a play or movie you would search the acting community to identify and cast the perfect actor for each role, selecting someone who will make the role come to life, someone who is dynamic, exciting, exuberant, interesting, and believable. Why is it that in the corporate world we tend to look for the candidates who have the best pedigrees, not for the ones who are interesting or diverse or have ideas that might be considered eccentric? Now, we realize that if you are on a pharmaceutical research new product development team, you need to have a fair share of "boring" Ph.D.s. But why not spice up the team with a wacky marketing type, or find one of those interesting Ph.D.s who took two years off to study alternative medicine in the Amazon?

Colorful, unique, memorable, magical moments will seldom be created by boring, myopic, unimaginative people!

Pixar hired director Brad Bird to shake things up because after three hits—*Toy Story, A Bug's Life,* and *Toy Story 2*—there was concern the company might struggle to continue creating new and freshly innovative films. Brad's first project was *The Incredibles.* Everything in this film was a nightmare for computer-generated animation—human characters, hair, water, fire, and a massive number of sets. Lasseter and the creative leads were ecstatic about the film, but the technical teams were about ready to go into coronary arrest. They told Brad that the project would take ten years and a mammoth budget to complete. Brad said, "Give us the 'black sheep.' I want artists who are frustrated. I want the ones who have another way of doing things that nobody's listening to. Give us all the guys who are probably headed out the door." Brad's "black sheep" were the malcontents who had been given little opportunity to try new ideas, since the first three films were such blockbusters. The "black sheep" stepped up to the challenge—and in the end, *The Incredibles* cost Pixar less per minute than its previous films while having three times the number of sets. The film won Academy Awards in 2005 for Best Animated Feature and Best Achievement in Sound Editing and was the highest-selling DVD of that year. Brad said, "All this because the heads of Pixar gave us leave to try crazy ideas."

Find your own team of malcontented, lunatic

fringe, wacky, "black sheep" dream makers!

Design the Backstage Processes

Imagine it is opening night of your Broadway play. You have an engaging, heartfelt, emotional story. You have an award-winning set designer and have assembled an ensemble of some of the best actors in the industry. You have rehearsed and rehearsed and rehearsed. Fantastic reviews will be forthcoming—or will they? What if duplicate tickets were sold, the curtain gets stuck halfway up, and the main stage lighting goes out during Act 3? What could have been a colossal hit might struggle to stay open.

Getting your "backstage" support and "onstage" disciplines to all work and play well together can be just as important to the success of your business as unleashing the creative energies within each department. Catmull maintains, "There always seems to be one function that considers itself and is perceived by others to be the one the organization values the most. In a creative business like ours, these barriers are impediments to producing great work, and therefore we must do everything in our power to tear them down. Walt Disney understood this. He believed that when continual change or reinvention is the norm—and [when] technology and art come together—magical things happen."

Hey, kids, let's put on a show! Get your creative team together to destroy that old sand castle and build a new one where customers' magical dream-come-true moments can happen every day.

Remove the barriers between "backstage"

processes and the "onstage" show,

and watch the magic happen!

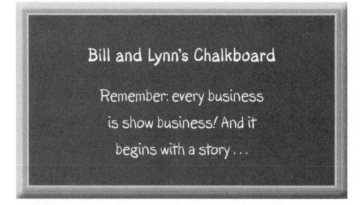

Bill and Lynn's Chalkboard

Remember: every business
is show business! And it
begins with a story . . .

4

Dream for Infinity and Beyond

The Beginnings of Pixar

WHEN WE WERE in first grade, we dreamed of being a fifth grader, and in middle school, we dreamed of being in high school. As children, we dream a lot about the future. But, typically, something happens to our childhood dreams as we grow up. One day, we find ourselves immersed in short-term strategies, dealing with quick-profit tactics—the dreams and dreamers just seem to disappear. Where are the Walt Disneys, the Sam Waltons, the Steve Jobses—those who pursued and succeeded in achieving their dreams?

Why are there so few examples of innovative organizations such as Disney, Wal-Mart, and Apple? Why instead does it appear we have amassed a growing list of scandalous corporations, the likes of AIG, Enron, and WorldCom? And as we write this book in 2009, we wonder what will be the fate of General Motors and the American banking system.

Much of this chaos is because short-term mentality has become a way of life. Fast food was not fast enough; we needed drive-through service. Paying with cash or with debit and credit cards was just too slow; we needed Speedpass. Immediate solutions and satisfaction are now required—for stock market investing, weight loss, loans, learning a language. The quick and easy lifestyle is the norm.

It is no different in the corporate world. A decade ago, the average tenure for a CEO was twelve years. Today it is less than five years. Wall Street expects a new CEO to have implemented a new strategy within the first one hundred days in office. So instead of taking the long-term view of investing in the future of a company, a new CEO begins to manipulate costs; eliminate jobs and training; ignore new markets and the customer; and compromise quality, all for the next quarter's earnings report.

Pursuing long-term results takes time, focus, and commitment. *Commitment* can be defined as "being intellectually or emotionally bound to a course of action." As an organization, Pixar has truly lived this definition and is staying the course, fulfilling long-term childhood dreams not only through intellectual pursuits but also with passion, spirit, and persistence. As Ed Catmull reflected, "Building an organization takes a long time. It takes a long time to learn how to do something right, and it also takes awhile to get the right people. In fact, one of the reasons Pixar has been successful is that we took our time building it."

In Salt Lake City's Granite High School, back in the early 1960s, Ed's dream was to become part of Disney's animation team. For Ed, seeing the artists drawing at their desks on the *Wonderful World of Disney* was exciting. But he soon realized his drawing skills were lacking and that he would never become a Disney animator. In later years, Ed admitted that he was a better artist than he had realized when he was in high school and may actually have made it as an animator—but there were no schools teaching animation at that time. With a keen aptitude for math and science, however, Ed turned his passion to the emerging world of computer graphics and refocused his dream: to make the first computer-animated feature film. Ed said, "When I took that first computer graphics course, then bam, it hit me . . . here's the art and the technology, and I reoriented everything around that, and the goal was to make the first [computer-] animated feature." When *Toy Story* was released in 1995, his dream became a reality.

This is a man who, despite having no one to teach him animation, was not deterred from his dream to use computer graphics in a theatrical playground, where art, science, and programming can be combined in harmonious symmetry. In the late 1960s, Ed landed at one of the world's preeminent seedbeds of computer graphics, the University of Utah, where he would earn undergraduate degrees in computer science and physics and a graduate degree in computer science.

Later, while working on his Ph.D., Ed discovered and developed technologies fundamental to the future of computer animation. One of his earliest contributions to the film industry resulted from a class project where he made a computer-animated rendering of his left hand. Hollywood took note. The hand appeared so realistic and the movement so natural that it was used in the 1976 science-fiction movie *Futureworld*, the very first film to utilize three-dimensional computer graphics.

And the rest is history—he moved up the ladder from director of the Computer Graphics Lab at the New York Institute of Technology (1974–1979) to vice president of the Computer Division of LucasFilms (1979–1986), to president of Pixar Animation Studios (1986–2006), and now president of Pixar and Disney Animation Studios (since 2006). Asked which of his accomplishments has made him the most proud, Ed responded, "That we have made the transition from researchers to storytellers."

It took Ed many years to accomplish his dream. He said, "For twenty years, I pursued a dream of making the first computer-animated film. To be honest, after that goal was realized—when we finished *Toy Story*—I was a bit lost. But then I realized the most exciting thing I had ever done was to help create the unique environment that allowed that film to be made." Nearly every step along the way was a challenge, to be sure, but Ed never gave up on his intellectual and emotional quest. Ed's genius stretches far beyond technology and innovation in filmmaking. He is also a master at discovering great talent. Two such star talents instrumental in realizing the dream of computer-generated films were Alvy Ray Smith and John Lasseter.

In describing his persona of the early 1970s, Alvy refers to himself as a "wild-ass hippie" who was thrilled by the idea of making pictures on computers and was just sort of hanging out waiting for a new and creative opportunity to strike his fancy. (Alvy is actually a brilliant mathematician and economist who wrote his doctoral thesis on automata theory.) At that time, computers could only generate monochromatic images. Then in 1974, Alvy paid a visit to his old friend and colleague Dick Shoup, who invented SuperPaint, a pioneering framebuffer computer system and graphics program that could handle color images, for which Dick won an Emmy in 1983. Dick showed Alvy around the computer science lab at the Xerox Palo Alto Research Center (PARC), where he developed SuperPaint. Alvy told us, "The moment I saw Dick Shoup's amazing machine, I knew how I was going to spend the rest of my life." Unable to convince the human resources department at PARC to hire Alvy (after all, in their minds, he was just an artist!), Dick actually submitted a purchase order to secure Alvy like a piece of equipment. Soon Alvy was getting paid to assist with further development of SuperPaint's features and began generating some of the very first color images on a computer. But the collegiate fun was about to end. In early 1975, Xerox announced that "Color is not part of the office of the future." Suddenly, Alvy found himself back on the street still looking to pursue his dream of producing computerized color animation. Shortly after being fired, he spoke to his University of Utah friend Martin Newell, who told him, "Perhaps you'd be interested to learn that a madman on Long Island has just been through the lab and bought a bunch of equipment including a framebuffer to make movies." (The framebuffer device is a direct ancestor of what we now call the graphics card, but as Alvy said, "It was two refrigerator-sized racks filled with equipment and, well, in today's dollars, probably cost a half million bucks.") Alvy remembers Martin telling him, "If I were you, I'd jump on the next plane. This guy's got everything, and he needs help."

Ed Catmull was already working for that Long Island "madman"—Alexander Shure, founder of the New York Institute of Technology. Alvy described his first meeting with Ed: "I saw this guy at a small metal desk and he spins around with *that look* . . . behind his short beard and glasses . . . and it was so clear his face said, 'God, do I need help.'" Alvy describes the small team of people who came together on the North Shore of Long Island as "just a bunch of guys and gals who saw that one of these days, we are going to be able to make movies, and let's be the first. We were collegiate. It wasn't money that drove us. It was academic fame." And that was the beginning of Pixar.

In the early 1980s, Ed and Alvy had met a young animator working at Disney Studios, John Lasseter, who impressed Alvy as being a bright kid who was not afraid of computers. In

1984, to Alvy's surprise, Ed phoned from a computer graphics conference on board the Queen Mary in Long Beach, California, to tell Alvy that John was no longer working for Disney. Alvy remembers telling Ed, "Get off the phone right now and hire him." And that's exactly what he did.

There are no accidents in the universe!

The final piece needed for accomplishing the dream of creating the first computer-animated feature film was in place. Alvy told us, "I could make things move [on the computer] but couldn't convince you they were alive and thinking. Animators are actors; they make you believe something that is not true. I've watched them for years and don't understand it at all. John was the best hire of my life. As you can see, we were putting all of the pieces in place."

Throughout his childhood years, John Lasseter loved cartoons more than anything else. During his freshman year at Whittier High School in California, he discovered a copy of Bob Thomas's *The Art of Animation*, which illustrates the facets of making animated feature films. This book changed John's life. Already a talented young artist who loved to draw pictures, make carvings, and create things out of plaster, John realized that he could really earn a living making cartoons. Right then and there, he cemented his dream of becoming a Disney animator.

John sent letters and drawings to the Disney Studios in an attempt to get them to recognize his talent. It worked. Ed Hansen, manager of Disney's animation department, invited him to tour the studio and encouraged young John to focus on getting a good, solid art education. In his senior year of high school, John opened a letter that would launch his long-term dream. CalArts, an art institute established in 1961 by Walt and Roy Disney, was beginning a new program in character animation. In short order, John submitted his portfolio, was accepted as the second enrollee, and became legendary program head Jack Hannah's (*Donald Duck* cartoon director) summer assistant. He had unlimited access to the Disney archives, which held all the treasures of animation—ones that he and his fellow students would use for study. John became a master of creative teaming, sharing story and project ideas, and playing critical evaluator with fellow students (including future Pixar film directors Chris Buck and Brad Bird)—a gift that would ultimately help him become a professional animator and an inspirational leader. At CalArts, he was blessed to have such iconic role models of creativity and leadership as Eric Larson, Frank Thomas, and Ollie Johnston—three of the famed "nine old men of Disney animation," the original animators who worked directly with Walt Disney beginning with *Snow White and the Seven Dwarfs* in 1937. Talk about dream makers!

But John himself was also a dream maker. He was beginning to set records; he was the first student ever to win two Student Academy Awards for making short films. One of the films, *The Lady and the Lamp*, showcased John's amazing gift for creating heartfelt animated stories starring inanimate objects that have the power to make people laugh and cry.

At the time of John's graduation from CalArts in 1979, Disney Studios was anxious to enlist John's creative talents, and he promptly accepted the challenge. On the new job, John began working on a project featuring animated hand-drawn characters against computer backgrounds. He believed that the computer was going to be the next great tool—following Walt Disney's multiplane camera—to create a three-dimensional effect. But trying to get the vast majority of Disney's veteran animators to accept the computer's true potential was nearly impossible. They believed the computer would destroy their careers.

Hoping to enlighten Disney executives, John sold them on the idea of developing an animated short feature called *The Brave Little Toaster*. After the artwork was completed, Ron Miller, head of Disney Studios, asked John how much the project would cost. When John told him that it would cost the same as any other Disney film, Miller replied that there was no point in using three-dimensional animation technology if it wasn't going to make things faster or cheaper. That same day, John's boss, Ed Hansen, told him, "Your project is now complete, so your employment with the Disney Studios is now terminated." Once again, rather than investing in the future and fostering creativity, Disney management, driven by short-term results, ignored the next wave of animated feature film technology and lost big.

Devastated by the dreadful news of being fired by Disney, John realized that despite being mentored by the remaining "nine old men of Disney animation," the senior creative leadership in the post-Walt era was anything but creative. What had happened to the Disney John had fallen in love with as a child? Where was Walt Disney's drive to "plus" everything he touched—transforming a scene or an attraction from good to great? Walt wasn't there to save the micromanaging suits from their relentless obsession with cost and speed of project delivery. Quality, as Walt Disney and John Lasseter defined it, was dead. Unbelievable, he thought. Within five short years, John's romance with Disney had fizzled out. But Disney's loss was soon to be Lucasfilm Computer Division's gain.

The partnership of Ed Catmull and John Lasseter has become one of the most symbiotic since that of Walt Disney and his brother Roy, who together opened the Disney Brothers Studio back in 1923. Like Walt and Roy, Ed and John have accomplished far beyond what either could have done alone. They all had what it takes to turn dreams into reality—in short, unshakable, long-lasting convictions, no matter the odds. In the words of Ed Catmull, "When we finished *Toy Story* . . . my new goal became, with John, to build a studio that had the depth, robustness, and the will to keep searching for the hard truths that preserve the confluence of forces necessary to create magic. . . . We've had the good fortune to expand that goal to include the revival of Disney Animation Studios. . . . But the ultimate test of whether John and I have achieved our goals is if Pixar and Disney are still producing animated films that touch world culture in a positive way long after we . . . are gone."

Their dreams realized, Ed Catmull and John Lasseter are now the pillars anchoring the empire that produces the most celebrated animated feature films of our time. The Pixar Animation Studio mission is evidence of their intertwined destinies, dreams that came true for two men: "to combine proprietary technology and world-class creative talent to develop computer-animated feature films with memorable characters and heartwarming stories that appeal to audiences of all ages." Dreams really can come true when you keep a long-term focus.

---

*Imagination is the bridge to reality when
you dream for infinity and beyond!*

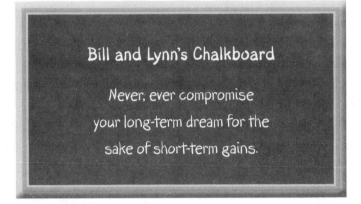

Bill and Lynn's Chalkboard

*Never, ever compromise
your long-term dream for the
sake of short-term gains.*

5
—

A New Way to Play "Follow the Leader"

REMEMBER PLAYING "FOLLOW the leader" as a child? The leader starts doing something—walk, run, dance, sing, or any activity the leader wants to do, in any order the leader chooses—and the rest of the players follow, doing exactly what the leader does. Anyone who doesn't exactly follow the leader is out of the game. The end of the game occurs when only one person remains following the leader. Of course, the leader's goal is to trick team members so they will be eliminated. Unfortunately, too many corporate managers play this game all too well. Rather than fostering an environment of self-motivated creative thinkers, they assume the role of pied piper, leading followers to drown in a river of corporate rules, regulations, and processes.

Walt Disney didn't ascribe to the childhood playbook for "follow the leader." We believe that some historians have misconstrued Walt's passion for requiring his animators to execute his bold ideas as micromanagement. In fact, he once said, "I am in no sense of the word a great artist, not even a great animator. I have always had men working for me whose skills were greater than my own. I am an idea man." It's true that Walt's dreams were aggressive—some even thought impossible—and his standards of excellence demanding. As we describe in our book *The Disney Way*, Walt's unique leadership definition made it possible to harness creative energies within his organization: "The ability to *establish* and *manage a creative climate* in which *individuals and teams* are *self-motivated* to the successful achievement of *long-term goals* in an environment of *mutual respect and trust*." In all our years of consulting, we have yet to discover a clearer and more enduring definition of exemplary leadership. Pixar is today's embodiment of Walt Disney's new "follow the leader" sentiment.

Establishment of a Clear Vision

Ed Catmull and Alvy Ray Smith put first things first by establishing Pixar with a clear vision and communicating that vision to its employees. The best leaders are excellent communicators. They engage their teams by providing them with the tools and information needed for success, and then trusting them to do their jobs. Alvy told us, "You can establish a company by fear or you can have a hierarchy that's by choice. You say, 'OK, you're good at that role. You can have it.' But still, you don't make arbitrary decisions. You consult [communicate] with the whole collegiate body and when you think you have them convinced and they all feel like it's the right decision to make, you make the decision."

Creative Climate

Managing a creative climate involves more than merely getting work done through people. Creative climates need leadership and a management style that helps them to develop and grow and allows them to have fun in the process. Let's examine the concepts of "development" and "fun." Pixar is clearly in the people development business— going to great lengths to nourish and support its employees (known as Pixarians). As a result, very few Pixarians ever consider leaving the company. It's the complete antithesis of the Hollywood contract worker model. Randy Nelson, dean of Pixar University, clearly renounces the industry's short-term staffing mentality: "It's generally the day you wrap production that you realize you've finally figured out how to work together. . . . Instead of investing in ideas, we invest in people. We're trying to create a culture of learning, filled with lifelong learners."

Indeed, as we'll illustrate in more detail later, every employee at Pixar—administrative, technical, management, janitorial, and security—is encouraged to pursue educational endeavors through Pixar University, Pixar's in-house employee development program. At Pixar University, you may even find president Ed Catmull himself in a class!

It's been proven that physical surroundings play a vital role in one's well-being, happiness, and creativity, and Pixar surely has taken this truth to heart. From the moment you glimpse the exterior of Pixar's sixteen-acre Emeryville, California, campus—dubbed "the Habitat"—it's clear that "establishing and managing a creative climate" was a carefully wrought plan. And it is arguably one of the finest testimonies to the fact that a childhood spirit is alive and well in corporate America. Even artists who freelance at Pixar gain inspiration from the building complex. Michel Gagné, who has worked on several Pixar projects over the years, told us, "I love the artist-friendly and noncorporate atmosphere. I find the architecture of the studio very conducive to creativity." The stage is set with Steve Jobs's inspired design of the curved metal roof resembling an airplane hangar, and the open-air "incredible-sized" atrium that serves as a "town square" for impromptu meetings, company celebrations, and just plain having fun. It's akin to a miniature Walt Disney World where unique employee dwellings, from tiki huts to castles, are fitting inspiration for their craft. You won't find any sterile hallways clustered with deadpan-faced workers whispering nervously about what happened in the Monday morning staff meeting. Not at Pixar. Pixarians are too busy inspiring one another with their storytelling, and when the mood strikes them, they stop by the atrium to engage a fellow team member in a game of foosball or enjoy a latte in the midst of life-sized Pixar characters. Step outside to spot them taking a dip in the Olympic-sized lap pool or strolling through the beautiful parklike campus. And, of course, there's a game room, with a new one under way in the four-story building currently in progress. When asked, "Why is it important to have a game room for people who make movies for a living?" Randy Nelson replied, "John Lasseter says the amount of fun the crew has in making the movie shows up in how much fun it is to watch. So play is a part of our work."

Individuals and Teams

Now, there's a whole lot more to producing a uniquely creative culture than simply putting up a fancy playground. Ed Catmull knows very well that creativity is a mental and social process that takes both individuals and teams. Ed emphasizes the importance of "set[ting] people up for success by giving them all the information they need to do the job right without telling them how to do it. Each person on the film must be given creative ownership of even the smallest task."

Pixar thrives on teamwork. Production teams set their own schedules and track all of the various aspects of the filmmaking process, even their own budgets. Naturally, there is enormous pressure to produce fresh and exciting stories—there's a solid story at the heart of every Pixar project, which takes approximately four years to bring to the big screen. It's a very disciplined process with project deadlines and delivery dates, but creativity is never squelched.

The level of cooperation at Pixar is amazing. The brain trust of Pixar's eight directors (Andrew Stanton, Brad Bird, Pete Docter, Bob Peterson, Brenda Chapman, Lee Unkrich, Gary Rydstrom, and Brad Lewis) and other team members who regularly provide value may spring into action on a moment's notice when a project is ready for feedback. Codirector Pete Docter shares how the review process worked on the 2009 blockbuster *Up* and others: "The way we work at Pixar is that we have our team that's making the film, and we get together about every four months and show it to other directors. I grab John Lasseter, Andrew Stanton, Brad Bird, and they all come in and watch the movie in whatever state it's in. And usually the first comments we get are about the characters. Carl, the main character in *Up*, was fun because he could be a jerk and likable at the same time. He could slam the door in the kid's face and you're like, 'Well, you know, he's earned that.'" It's hard to imagine that a group with this much brain power is restricted to giving advice only! Indeed, it's totally up to the director and the team to decide what's going to end up in a Pixar film.

The practice of delivering honest feedback is not limited to the directors and producers. At most movie studios, the daily review of works-in-process, termed the "dailies," is reserved for a small group of senior staff only. At Pixar, the entire team shares its unfinished work each day with any Pixarian who wants to attend. Ed Catmull feels there are several benefits to this practice. First, once the team members get over the embarrassment of presenting an unfinished product, they become more creative. Second, the director has the opportunity to communicate important story concepts to the entire company. Third, people are inspired and energized by the creative work of others. And finally, there are no surprises at the end. This level of autonomy and accountability can never happen in a fear-based culture. As Ed said, "Creativity doesn't follow titles; it just comes from where it comes from."

Self-Motivated Personnel

Great leaders know that self-motivated people are essential to developing a creative culture. The late management guru Peter Drucker once wrote, "Ninety percent of what we call management consists of making it difficult for people to get things done." Think about this. If you go to great lengths to hire the right person for a job; provide a thorough understanding of the culture of the organization through an orientation process that explains the vision and values of the company; and provide systematic, on-the-job training and ongoing educational opportunities for all employees, why on earth would you need to micromanage anyone? Disney, Google, and other high-performing organizations filled with self-motivated people experience spans of control greater than 20:1. That means one manager for more than twenty workers. In most U.S. companies, the span of control is less than 8:1.

At Pixar, it is hard to calculate the span of control. In the first place, no organizational chart is consulted when it comes to solving problems, and more important, everyone resides within an environment that is totally open. Pixarians have the freedom to communicate with anyone in the organization regardless of level or title. Ed explains, "This means recognizing that the decision-making hierarchy and communication structure in organizations are two different things. Members of any department should be able to approach anyone in another department to solve problems without having to go through 'proper' channels. It also means that managers need to learn that they don't always have to be the first to know about something going on in their realm, and it's OK to walk into a meeting and be surprised."

Ed continually scouts for new talent that can blossom within Pixar's unique culture, and he has a knack for finding the best. Ed recalled, "One of my first hires [at New York Institute of Technology] was Alvy Ray Smith, who made breakthroughs in computer painting. That made me realize that it's OK to hire people who are smarter than you are." Hiring the right people is critical to the success of any organization, but few leaders are comfortable hiring people who might actually be smarter than they are. Early in his career, Ed was convinced that creativity can flow in all directions when people aren't hung up on who is smarter or who has the best idea. Pixarians are 100 percent self-motivated to being as creative as they can be and to making movies the best they can. Period.

Long-Term Goals

The folks at Pixar are focused on long-term goals. As director Brad Bird stated, "It's never been about cheaper [and] faster at Pixar. It's creating for the long term. People here love the characters, and they're aware that these films, if done correctly, are living things." As was true of Walt Disney, Pixar has a definition of "long-term" that speaks volumes about its culture—they go to great lengths to ensure that its culture can support new ventures and still remain true to their values.

Mutual Respect and Trust

Pixar employees have embarked on a journey together, nurturing one another in an environment of mutual respect and trust—perhaps the most important aspect of our leadership definition.

Merriam-Webster's Collegiate Dictionary defines *respect* as "to consider worthy of high regard"; and *trust* as "to place confidence in or rely on someone or something." Great leaders seek individuals with unique talents who are willing to work with them, not for them—although having a talented staff isn't enough. As Catmull explained, "What's equally tough, of course, is getting talented people to work effectively with one another. That takes trust and respect, which we as managers can't mandate. They must be earned over time." When leaders exhibit this level of respect and trust, that's exactly what they get in return.

Catmull and Lasseter are really more of a "heart trust" than a "brain trust." Their "share the spotlight" management style has created a safe haven where employees are accountable to one another. As Alvy Ray Smith told us, the two of them are a "technical and artistic collaboration of the first order. . . . It's because they both have great respect for one another. They both know that they couldn't do what the other does, and couldn't do without what the other does."

The power of the collaborative spirit at Pixar cannot be overstated. And certainly, Ed's belief in his team is evident in his words: "If you give a good idea to a mediocre team, they'll screw it up. But if you give a mediocre idea to a great team, they'll make it work." He also demonstrates his trust in employees by refusing to institute employment contracts, as he believes that such a display of corporate control and power is the antithesis of a culture where open channels of communication are imperative.

Pixar is a place where the stories spring to life, one beat at a time, and the characters and relationships become real. It's a war-room approach to storytelling, where electric excitement fills the air with bantering and laughing, and where individuals and teams are engaged with one another in the process of playing out each other's ideas. That's an environment of mutual respect and trust.

There's no "follow the leader" game of childish trickery at Pixar. The playbook simply calls for an open playground where leadership serves as a catalyst in the pursuit of big dreams.

"The things we live by and teach our children are preserved or diminished by how freely we exchange ideas and feelings."

—Walt Disney

Bill and Lynn's Chalkboard

Leadership may be boiled down to the Golden Rule: "Do unto others as you would have them do unto you." List all the things you hated that leaders have done to you. Do not do these to others! Next list all the things you loved that leaders have done to you. Do these to others!

BELIEVE IN YOUR PLAYMATES

6

Collaboration
in the Sandbox

HAVE YOU EVER watched the interplay of children in a sandbox? The younger ones watch with curiosity how the older children build their sandcastles. From time to time, the older children will mentor the younger ones, suggesting ideas and providing instruction for using the essential construction tools—shovels and buckets. Kids don't need to take "Sandcastle Building 101" to learn how to build a sandcastle. They learn from intense observation and by trial and error in a collaborative environment.

In 1887, after only two semesters, the legendary architect Frank Lloyd Wright left the University of Wisconsin–Madison. It wasn't long before he went to Chicago to meet with Louis Sullivan, father of the modern-day skyscraper, and told him that he wanted to become an architect. Sullivan was impressed with the young man and hired him. On his first day of work, Wright asked him, "What should I do?" Sullivan told him to sit down and watch. In later years, Wright opened his own college where students learned through watching other architects and assisting on real projects, just the way Sullivan instructed Wright and just like in the sandbox.

Walt Disney once said, "Every child is born blessed with a vivid imagination. But just as a muscle grows flabby with disuse, so the bright imagination of a child pales in later years if he ceases to exercise it." Truly creative people exhibit a level of enthusiasm for imagination and discovery that harkens back to the days of childhood. Indeed, innovation begins with a beginner's mind and is often stimulated by a catalyst.

Merriam-Webster's defines *catalyst* as "an agent that provokes or speeds significant change or action." For Frank Lloyd Wright, that agent was Louis Sullivan. For Ed Catmull, it was his two childhood idols—Walt Disney and Albert Einstein. For John Lasseter, it was Bob Thomas's book, *The Art of Animation*, about the history of the Disney Studios. For Randy Nelson, it was Ed Catmull and a memo written by Walt Disney that inspired the creation of Pixar University. And for the kids in the Tucson Unified School

District (TUSD), it is the now nationally recognized Opening Minds through the Arts (OMA) program.

Pixar University and the Tucson Unified School District's OMA program are both catalysts that encourage educational change in their respective worlds of corporate America and the U.S. public school system. Seemingly worlds apart, they share a long-term commitment to a learning process that encourages collaborative creativity. They both have "champions" of their respective learning models and, in their own unique ways, make art a team sport.

At the completion of *Toy Story*, Pixar's Ed Catmull and John Lasseter began discussions on the importance of continuing education in building a top-notch studio—one in which not only new employees could learn the skills they need, but also veteran staff could expand their learning horizons beyond their fields of expertise, and a place where everyone would learn collaboratively. Like Walt Disney before them, Ed and John planned a studio-based school, and they sought out a leader who was not an artist in the traditional sense of the word. Pixar University (John said, "We picked the name just for its initials, P.U.") was soon to be under the direction of Randy Nelson, a former technical trainer at NeXT (founded in 1985 by Steve Jobs) and one of the founding members of the world-famous juggling troupe the Flying Karamazov Brothers. It stands to reason, if you are going to offer a highly diverse array of courses, why not hire a guy with a highly diverse background as the leader? As Ed said, "He had an unusual combination of skills, which I felt was an asset. I figured I'd rather have a world-class juggler running the program than a mediocre artist. People who have experience doing great work understand something that can be applied to other things."

Walt Disney's studio-based school of the 1930s was the inspiration for Pixar University nearly a half century later. Walt once said, "I think we shouldn't give up until we have found out all we can about how to teach these young [people]. . . . There are a number of things that could be brought up in these discussions to stir [their] imagination, so that when they get into actual animation, they're not just technicians, but they're actually creative people." This was a key message in the eight-page memo Walt Disney wrote to Don Graham (legendary art instructor at Chouinard Art Institute in downtown Los Angeles and author of *Composing Pictures*, an out-of-print classic coveted by both art students and animators) just before Christmas in 1935. At that time, Walt was planning the production of *Snow White and the Seven Dwarfs* and needed to hire and train new animators in short order. In his memo, he outlined "a very systematic training course for young animators, and also outlined a plan of approach for [our] older animators." With Walt's detailed plan for developing the finest artists in the industry, Don Graham carried forth the creation of a curriculum that included courses on drawing, comedy, music, dialogue, and motion, and intertwined them in a holistic fashion, as Walt described, "to stir up the men's minds more."

The now famous Walt Disney memo would remain at Disney for decades, eventually falling into the hands of Ed Catmull, John Lasseter, and Randy Nelson. Walt's missive inspired and motivated them. Since being crowned dean of Pixar University in 1997 (Randy says he's a "fake" dean and "at the same level as the guy at McDonald's Hamburger University"), Randy Nelson has gone from juggling knives on Broadway to juggling an extensive lineup of courses (and is still juggling foot-long knives in gesture-drawing class at P.U.!) that rivals some of the finest public institutions offering art degrees. With more than 110 courses on everything from improv to the Israeli self-defense system Krav Maga, "Big Art"—the boxy brick building that is home to P.U.—is always buzzing. And don't let Randy's charismatic persona fool you. He's fun, to be sure, but he is dead serious about integrating learning opportunities into the work lives of Pixar's approximately 1,000 employees. "We're all film-makers here," says Randy. "We all have access to the same curriculum. In class, people from every level sit right next to our directors and the president of the company." So passionate about building a strong base of "interested" people, Pixar challenges employees to dedicate up to four hours of every single week to their education. Pixar University has been a vital catalyst for employees who are encouraged to take a great deal of responsibility for their own learning and for collaborating with one another. Randy maintains that "the skills we develop are skills we need everywhere in the organization. Why teach drawing to accountants?

Because drawing class doesn't just teach people to draw. It teaches them to be more observant. There's no company on earth that wouldn't benefit from having people become more observant."

Walt Disney felt each person in his company should "plus" another's ideas to make them bigger, even better. Pixar has certainly "plus-ed" Walt Disney's idea for a "little" art school. Since its inception in 1995, Pixar University has truly lived up to its reputation as a "secret weapon"—one that challenges, in Steve Jobs's words, "the densest group of really brilliant people that I've ever seen in my life" to continue to push the boundaries of their art.

If you set out to develop a plan for creating a learning environment for children to prepare them for working in an environment such as Pixar, you'd surely be benchmarking the OMA project in Tucson, Arizona. In less than a decade, what began as one man's dream of integrating the arts into the entire learning experience within a single school district is now the cutting edge of a new paradigm in public education.

OMA was created around children's neurological development and brain-based learning theories. The program employs teaching artists—professionals from Tucson's cultural institutions—who use music, dance, and visual arts to teach concepts and skills applied in academic subjects like reading, writing, math, and science. Carroll Reinhart, OMA cofounder, said, "What I get excited about with the OMA project is that I see artists helping classroom teachers helping principals to understand the very essence of what art is." The curriculum is designed to engage specific skills targeted to each grade level, and the results have been amazing. Since 2001, OMA has been working with WestEd, a nationally recognized educational research firm, to conduct a study comparing three "research" schools that were fully implementing the OMA model and three "control" schools that were utilizing standard teaching methodology. WestEd's research focused on answering two primary questions: does OMA have a positive effect on test results in reading, writing, and math; and does OMA improve teacher effectiveness? The answer to both was a resounding "yes."

When Bill observed the OMA program, he was particularly impressed by the first-grade opera experience. For the first half of the year, students learn opera by watching members of the Tucson Opera perform a short opera, and then performing the same parts themselves. During the second half of the year, the students write their own opera and perform it as their final class project. These are *first* graders! One of the first-grade OMA lesson plans reads like a Pixar University course description: "Use Beethoven's song 'The Mighty Monarch' to teach students sequencing through two different means—first, by explaining the writing process (poet, composer, performer), and then by using the characters and the sequence of the story." What a way to begin an educational journey!

Not only are OMA students being exposed to the art form of opera, but these children also learn vocabulary, story construction, collaboration, and "failure recovery" while having fun. It's a lot like the sandbox or the Frank Lloyd Wright example—observe, try, learn, and try again within a supportive team. According to Rick Wamer, OMA program coordinator, "OMA creates an environment in the school where the children feel safe to risk making mistakes and recover from those mistakes in the process of inquiry and exploration. They come to understand that that's not crippling, but somehow we build mastery through that." The children of OMA courageously explore and share new ideas with one another, with the belief that other students' ideas are assets in the exploration process. In short, they learn that more knowledge, creativity, and ideas can be found in two minds than in one, and that even more can be found in five or ten. Rick explained, "What I think is so valuable at OMA has to do with core values. . . . It's completely opposed to the typical assessment and evaluation of children being evaluated on how I answer these questions in a multiple-choice fashion on this piece of paper."

Steve Seidel, director of Harvard University's Project Zero (whose stated mission is "to understand and enhance learning, thinking, and creativity in the arts, as well as humanistic and scientific disciplines, at the individual and institutional levels"), recently said, "OMA had better be ready to grow, because in a few years, this will be the standard by which all other programs will be judged, and it will be the model for the entire country." He spoke these words to J. Eugene "Gene" Jones, the founding "dreamer" and major champion of OMA who is now a retired entrepreneur after earning a fortune turning around troubled companies. The 93-year-old Gene focuses his enormous energy into two of his lifelong passions: music and education. As incoming president of the Tucson Symphony in 2000, Gene attended an annual symphony leadership meeting in North Carolina and happened to stumble upon a class where the music director was using music as a classroom educational tool. After walking through that door and watching the creativity and energy pouring forth from the children, he said to himself, "If that is what music will do, that's what we are damn well going to do and do it better." His passion for creating an innovative arts-education program in his own community was so great that he donated more than $1 million of his own money to launch OMA, which currently operates in more than half of Tucson's elementary schools and a quarter of its middle schools.

Joan Ashcraft, director of fine and performing arts at TUSD and cofounder of OMA, said, "I was so grateful to have Gene Jones say to me, 'Just do it. . . . Find people that support your dreams.'" Roger Pfeuffer, former superintendent of TUSD, said that it was imperative that the "dream" team challenge the local naysayers who feared "bringing a Cadillac model to a Chevrolet town." Roger—who clearly understood the immense value of an arts integration curriculum in developing fully functioning individuals—explained, "The OMA model isn't an add-on; it's got to be part of the core. You've also got to have a long-term view, what is needed in higher education and beyond." And as

OMA cofounder Jan Vesely added, "We integrated art and music into the learning because I believe that higher-order thinking comes when you integrate."

Today, the cofounders and champions of OMA—Gene Jones, Joan Ashcraft, Carroll Rinehart, Jan Vesely, and John Snavely—remain fully engaged in building a world-class educational arena where an "art is a team sport" culture facilitates student achievement and social growth. "Our district is taking on the amazing challenge of moving OMA to the next level . . . designing the learning that will meet the future needs of our 'digital native' students," says superintendent Elizabeth Fagen. And who knows? They may also be preparing the future generation of Pixarians!

"Art is a team sport" is the very essence of learning and working in a collaborative fashion at Pixar. Pixar encourages employees to share their ideas and art-in-process, and to accept feedback from others without worrying about being labeled a failure. Fittingly, the Pixar University crest bears the inscription "Alienus Non Diutius," Latin for "alone no longer." "It's the heart of our model," Randy Nelson says, "giving people opportunities to fail together and to recover from mistakes together." Remember—this is an environment of mutual respect and trust, two vital ingredients required for innovation in teams. As Ed Catmull, whose leadership sets the tone for Pixar's culture of safe risk taking, said, "Everyone at the company will tell you there are no bad ideas at Pixar, even if they don't end up in a movie." And when it comes to developing new stories and technologies, Ed humbly admits, "We're constantly figuring it out. We don't have all the answers." But, with a workforce of truly interested people who band together and constantly explore new ways to fulfill their dreams, it is clearly apparent why Pixar continues to succeed.

Pixar goes to great lengths to hire people who are interested in working together as a "network . . . in solving problems, building and supporting each other," as Ed describes it. Four common proficiencies—depth, breadth, communication, and collaboration—are vital to making "art a team sport."

Here are definitions of these proficiencies according to Randy Nelson:

- ◆ **Depth**—demonstrating mastery in a subject or a principal skill such as drawing or programming; having the discipline to chase dreams all the way to the finish line.
- ◆ **Breadth**—possessing a vast array of experiences and interests; having empathy for others; having the ability to explore insights from many different perspectives; and being able to effectively generate new ideas by collaborating with an entire team. Randy described people who have breadth: "They amplify *you*. They want to know what *you* want to know." In problem solving, they are the ones who lean in, rather than pulling back.
- ◆ **Communication**—focusing on the receiver; receiving feedback to ascertain whether the message sent was truly understood. According to Randy, "Com-

munication is not something the emitter can measure." Only the listener can say, "I understand."

♦ **Collaboration**—bringing together the skills (including depth, breadth, and communication), ideas,
and personality styles of an entire team to achieve a
shared vision. "Yes, and . . ." (rather than "No, this is
better") is part of Pixar's common lexicon that fosters
collective creativity and keeps the vibe and energy in
the room upbeat and alive.

Collaboration is critical to the process of generating ideas
and solving problems in any organization. At Pixar, there
are literally thousands of ideas that are considered during
the making of a film. As Catmull explained, "Everyone is
trying to solve these problems, and a lot of ideas are thrown
out there that don't work. . . . You get in a group of people,
they look at it, you get ideas . . . and you come back and you
make the performance better. . . . If you think about it, this
is creative problem solving."

Those who gain mastery in anything have become
comfortable with the process of failure recovery. From
the technicians to the artists, these gifted and talented
team members have needs and concerns that emerge
from "errors" in their independent work—ones that motivate them to seek solutions. Sharing breadth, however,
leads them to collaborate with others to do so. In truly
living the Pixar University mantra of "alone no longer,"

employees do not struggle in isolation. When team members come together to find a solution to a problem, they are energized and strive to discover creative options for accomplishing their goals. They don't get trapped into thinking that an answer is the *only* answer.

Pixarians working in a team environment (standard operating procedure at Pixar) are open to alternative answers helping foster an outward focus. They understand that an outward focus is a requirement for seeking and accepting new inputs and ideas in a playground where "art is a team sport." As John Lasseter stated, "Pixar is actively expanding its talent base. We have younger filmmakers experiment with ideas and technology. The next thing you know, we have assigned them to come up with feature ideas." When asked about the process of making *Up*, codirector Pete Docter said, "This is a very personal film, yet it's intensely collaborative. No one person could do this. . . . So as a director . . . [I don't] tell them too specifically what I want. 'On frame seven, I want him to grab the bottle.' It's more the feeling, 'Remember, he's just run seven miles. He's exhausted, he's angry.' Just tell [the animators] those sorts of details and think of them more like an actor. Let them bring their ideas to the thing."

Pixar employees care enough about one another and are emotionally secure enough, as Randy Nelson explained, to make their "partner(s) look good." Team members continually "plus" one another's work—all in the spirit of sorting through and refining a multitude of ideas that gel together to produce, in the words of Ed Catmull, a "wonderful magical whole."

Pixar's really magical stories come to life through the able hands of *interested* people—a quality Randy says is much more valuable than simply being *interesting*. How, you may ask, do we cultivate the gift of being truly *interested*—opening the mind to new ideas and possibilities, persistently seeking answers to questions, and digging deep to find the best solutions to problems? Pixar University's model of education enables employees to do just that.

We wonder what it will take to change the culture of formal education that all too often stifles the imaginations of children and adults alike. We must leave behind the culture of answering questions *correctly* and adopt a culture of safe inquiry, exploration, and discovery. OMA's Rick Wamer is in sync with Pixar president Ed Catmull in building a culture where try, learn, and try again—failure recovery—is integral to making "art a team sport." Rick explained, "The process of artistic inquiry is exploration and discovery, and it's making mistakes a million thousand times, and it's throwing away a million thousand things that you come to . . . and saving and valuing specific things out of this pool of things you discover. That's what you hold on to as an artist and [what] is ultimately woven into the content of any kind of product you create."

As is true of Pixar, the advantage in this world will always go to *interested* people who can outcollaborate and outinnovate their competitors—and the fully engaged OMA children will someday be ready to do just that! Choose your sandbox. Will it set the stage for opening minds through experiential collaborative learning opportunities or merely opening minds and pouring in the facts?

"I happen to be an inquisitive guy and when I see things I don't like, I start thinking why do they have to be like this and how can I improve them."

—Walt Disney

Bill and Lynn's Chalkboard

Innovation does not come from a miraculous revelation on the road to Damascus. It comes from habitual, nonstop collaboration!

7

Stand Together Against the Bullies

ASK ANY GROUP of children to name the bullies at their school, and they won't need to guess. Most can point out the bad guys without hesitation. There's always someone bigger and stronger, tougher and meaner, who relishes being the proverbial leader of the pack. Bullies are particularly adept at calculating how to best exercise their power and inflict pain on others. Any child on the receiving end of such abuse runs the risk of developing low self-esteem, getting poor grades, and perhaps even living an unfulfilled life.

Remember the old adage "there's safety in numbers"? Bullies know very well that it's a lot harder to fight the whole pack than a single straggler. The savvy kids are quick to figure out that it's best to form a coalition and stand strong.

When we finally arrive in the corporate world, we often discover that some of those early lessons in life still hold true. In many organizations, bullying comes in the form of kick butt and take names or command and control management. And the result for employees can be virtually the same as for kids back in the schoolyard—depression, poor performance, and just plain going through the motions of a thankless job. We've all known those intimidating, title-seeking managers who impose unrealistic demands and change the rules at a moment's notice without rational justification.

There are lessons to be learned from Pixar's animation leaders about dealing with such bullies. In the 1990s, Pixar got its big break when it signed a three-picture deal with Walt Disney Studios, the first film being *Toy Story*. However, John Lasseter, the late Joe Ranft, Pete Docter, and Andrew Stanton found themselves under the thumb of one of Hollywood's most notable bullies—the volatile Jeffery Katzenberg, then head of Walt Disney Studios.

The *Toy Story* team was inspired to bring to life a story about buddies—guys who might have had a rocky start to their relationship but who became friends for a greater cause. After going through several transformations, the writers finally modeled the main character—Woody—after

Woody Strode, a cowboy actor who costarred in several John Wayne movies.

Yet, Lasseter and his team had to endure constant nit-picking from Katzenberg about the story and were forced to adhere to a tight schedule regardless of the quality that resulted. Not even Peter Schneider, then senior vice president of Disney Feature Animation and responsible for seeing the project through to completion, could protect the team from the bullying leader of the pack. Katzenberg, who sat through briefings on the yet-to-be-titled story, was annoyed with Woody's "childlike" persona and called for the character to have more "edge." This meant the team would need to kill their original idea and transform Woody into a cruel character who they believed would fail to touch the heartstrings of moviegoers. Surely, no one would cheer for such a jerk in the end!

A number of very painful weeks ensued during which the team was forced to continue down a path of near destruction of their original story idea. When Lasseter sat through a screening of the original film and witnessed how dark Woody's character had become, he shuddered to think of what he himself had become. He had allowed someone else to derail him on his journey of making a really great film with endearing characters—and much more than that—to steal his passion. John was on the brink of destroying the movie that he and his buddies had set out to make.

When Katzenberg got wind of the Lasseter team's righteous indignation, he demanded that the film's production be halted immediately. He further insisted that Pixar reduce the size of its crew and ordered the story team to pack their bags and move to Disney headquarters so that he could manage the process on his own turf.

The team knew their battle had reached the final stage. They balked at the thought of moving in with "the enemy." It was now a matter of whether they were willing to make a movie they didn't really like. In the words of director Andrew Stanton (*Finding Nemo, WALL-E, John Carter of Mars* [2012]), "We really went through boot camp to learn how to make *Toy Story* under Katzenberg's regime. . . . I mean, you were told, 'This is exactly how you do it,' and so we were basically thrown into the pool and forced to learn how to swim. But the detriment was that every little decision was being forced on us, from the kinds of jokes we should tell and the manner in which something should happen all the way down to the nitty-gritty details. This was this whole new world of making a feature, so we deferred to the big boys, but in the process, we sort of let Woody's character slip past us."

How could they let this happen—sell their dreams out to someone else's demands? The team decided to present their case for developing the original story idea. "Just give us two weeks," John pleaded, "and we'll turn things around." Amazingly, their request was granted.

In the end, Disney executives were dazzled by the way the team worked day and night to deliver a rework of the film where Woody emerged as a more sympathetic leader. Even Katzenberg's futile arrogance evaporated when he attended a screening of the reworked film. He was pleasantly surprised that the team had actually infused the story with some of his own ideas. (Katzenberg would later partner with Steven Spielberg and David Geffen to form DreamWorks.)

The making of *Toy Story* was a process that took many heart-pounding twists and turns, not only in the development of the film itself but also in the team dynamics of Pixar's inner circle of creative genius. John Lasseter and his team came to realize that they had been tested by a formidable opponent, and they also learned there was no limit to what they could accomplish together. Just think of how different Pixar might be today if the team had allowed Katzenberg's bullying to derail their dream.

Pixar's founding values of collaboration and mutual respect were solidified during the process of making *Toy Story*. As Pixar cofounder Alvy Ray Smith explained to us, "If you are going to have a really talented group of people, it's really important to have mutual respect and dignity across the technical and graphical divide."

Creative people flourish when they unite to forge new frontiers and when they refuse to compromise their values—even if it means pushing back on unyielding, high-ranking corporate bullies. To avoid constant interference from bullies in suits, it's important to establish specific milestones within your projects and invite the "suits" to a briefing or two. These milestones have three purposes: first, to present the current status and results achieved thus far; second, to continue selling the "dream"; and third, to gain management input. Remember to treat management as you would treat a customer—focus on getting them to embrace your dreams.

Now, you may be thinking, "But we could lose our jobs!" And, maybe for some, the potential reward is just not worth the risk. But the downside risk might be even greater—the dream of a lifetime could slip away.

"I'm not interested in pleasing the critics.

I'll take my chances pleasing the audiences."

—Walt Disney

Bill and Lynn's Chalkboard

Remember: what is right isn't always popular, and what is popular isn't always right. Let your values be your guide!

DARE TO JUMP IN THE WATER AND MAKE WAVES

8

The Skater Who Never Falls Will Never Win the Gold!

MANY YEARS AGO when Bill's youngest son, Tony, was four, he began taking ice-skating lessons. Bill remembers watching the first lesson when all the other little four-year-olds were carefully taking tiny steps trying to skate from one end of the rink to the other without falling down—but not Tony. He would take a giant glide and become airborne with his skates pointing to the sky and his bottom hitting the ice. He would quickly get up and try again, this time taking two or three giant glides before launching into the sky. This trial-and-error session continued for about fifteen minutes, with Tony staying on his skates a little longer each time before falling. By the end of the lesson, the other four-year-olds were still taking tiny steps, and Tony was skating with only an occasional spill. By the time he turned eighteen, Tony was so good that he skated professionally at Six Flags Magic Mountain in Valencia, California.

Remember, when we were very young, we would naturally *try, learn,* and *try again.* Sadly, our natural ability to do this—to trip and fall without fear of criticism—is over in a flash. Fear of failure can stop success right in its tracks.

While in school, we are often educated into believing that we must succeed—that mistakes should be avoided. But to be successful, we need to learn how to fail and how to respond to failure. What we call failure is really a learning process. Randy Nelson, dean of Pixar University, shares this healthy view of failure with his students: "You have to honor failure, because failure is just the negative space around success." Successful people think of failure as a learning method to propel themselves toward success.

Failures?
- The fax machine was a failed invention in the 1840s.
- The copy machine was rejected by GE and IBM in 1937, finally being produced in 1947.
- John Grisham's first novel was rejected by twelve publishers.
- Henry Ford went bankrupt five times.

- Vincent Van Gogh sold only one painting during his lifetime.
- Orville Wright was expelled from elementary school.
- The Chicago Cubs have not won a World Series since 1908. (For some, it takes longer than others!)
- Michael Jordan once failed to make his high school varsity basketball team.
- Oprah Winfrey failed as a news reporter.
- Winston Churchill finished last in his class.

J. K. Rowling, the first billion-dollar author, was a jobless, single mom on welfare when she wrote her first Harry Potter book. According to Rowling, "It is impossible to live without failing at something, unless you lived so cautiously that you might as well not [have] lived at all—in which case you failed by default." Failing forward is about learning from our mistakes—examining failures and moving beyond them to achieve success. In today's business world, companies need to fail forward fast, and that learning at a faster pace requires making mistakes at a faster pace. But it's not always easy when a whole team or even a whole company gets off track and nearly misses a big "win" because they didn't learn fast enough.

Pixar president Ed Catmull has made risk taking a key link in the company's chain of most enduring values. "We as executives have to resist our natural tendency to avoid or minimize risks, which, of course, is much easier said than done—this instinct leads executives to choose to copy successes rather than try to create something brand-new.

That's why you see so many movies that are so much alike. It also explains why a lot of films aren't very good. If you want to be original, you have to accept the uncertainty, even when it's uncomfortable, and have the capability to recover when your organization takes a big risk and fails."

Creativity demands awareness—attention to managing the failures that happen on the path to success. The reason this is such a daunting task for most organizations is that they bog down in bureaucracy—hoping and praying a problem won't turn into a crisis or going on a witch hunt to find someone to blame. Creative people learn that failure really is, as Randy Nelson put it, "that negative space around success."

Here are ten ideas to encourage risk taking and a "try, learn, and try again" culture:

1. Celebrate failure with the same intensity that you celebrate success.

2. Become a prototype junky—there is no project too big that you shouldn't be able to conduct a real-world test of it within a few weeks.

3. Develop your own "skunk works"—teams given a high degree of autonomy and disencumbered by bureaucracy. (*Skunk works* is a term coined by Ben Rich and Kelly Johnson while working at Lockheed in 1943.) Don't rely on corporate resources to complete your prototype; beg,

borrow, or steal material, tools, and expertise to complete it.

4. **Dream BIG.** Ask each team member to think of ten over-the-top, outlandish, eccentric, far-out, wacky, unheard-of, unorthodox ideas for your project. If they each can't come up with ten ideas, recruit more idiosyncratic thinkers who continue to try over-the-top ideas. Even if these ideas fail—learn, and try again.

5. **Don't cry poor.** Many innovative breakthroughs haven't come from the formal "fat cats" in the R&D departments but from field operations scrounging around trying something new, learning, and trying again. Not having the budget is an excuse, not a barrier!

6. **Planning is OK, but don't become a slave to the plan.** General George Patton once said, "A good plan today is better than a perfect plan next week." A plan must be flexible enough to allow many tries and retries.

7. **Use a "planning center" approach to track your plans.** A planning center is a place where a team's plans and prototypes are visually displayed and tracked.

8. **Forget about long planning meetings and reports.** Walking into the planning center should give team members and management the current status on the project.

9. It is easier to ask for forgiveness than permission. Assume authority. Quickly review and record failures, then within forty-eight hours, try again. In most organizations, getting permission to try again takes countless meetings, reports, approvals, and often inquisitions to find the person responsible for the "failure."

10. You need a soul mate. Find a customer or supplier who is just as outlandish and daring as your team to help test and refine your prototypes and ideas.

Ed Catmull knows well that innovation is all about taking risks, as is evidenced by his comment, "When something goes wrong, we respond to the thing that goes wrong, but we don't try to prevent it from going wrong by not doing something risky in the first place. So we start off scared, and we stay scared until we're done." Go out on the ice and take those giant glides—you may fall, but sooner or later, you will be doing triple axels.

Full speed ahead, as fast as you can—

try, learn, and try again.

Bill and Lynn's Chalkboard

Failure can be exciting. It captures the imagination. But . . . you've got to fail at the speed of change. And when you do, rejoice and learn!

9

Recess

Go Out and Play!

CHILDREN LAUGHING, BALLS bouncing, hopscotch courts, baseball diamonds—the sounds and sights of the playground. We all remember them, but will these childhood memories share the same destiny as drugstore soda fountains and 45 rpm records? What has happened to play time? The national affiliate of the International Play Association (IPA/USA) actively promotes the right to play. In fact, IPA/USA's purpose is "to protect, preserve, and promote play as a fundamental right for all humans" as established by the United Nations Convention on the Rights of the Child, Article 31. Yet according to IPA/USA, "Within the United States, 40% of schools do not provide our children with recess." We find this statistic appalling and were shocked to learn there is a need for an international association to protect our right to play! It's just a miracle that any company is innovative when so many of our educational institutions have eliminated arguably the greatest learning enhancer in the public school system—RECESS.

Since 1926, the National Association for the Education of Young Children (NAEYC) has been dedicated to improving the lives of children. NAEYC cites several reasons school administrators should carefully consider the benefits of play before eliminating recess:

- Play is an active form of learning that unites the mind, body, and spirit. Until at least the age of nine, children's learning occurs best when the whole self is involved.
- Play reduces the tension that often comes with having to achieve or needing to learn. In play, adults do not interfere and children relax. They return to the classroom ready to learn and be productive.
- Children express and work out emotional aspects of everyday experiences through unstructured play.
- Children permitted to play freely with peers develop skills for seeing another person's point of view—cooperating, helping, sharing, and solving problems.
- The development of children's perceptual abilities may suffer when so much of their experience is through television, computers, books, worksheets, and media that require only two senses. The senses

of smell, touch, and taste and the sense of motion through space are powerful modes of learning.

◆ Children who are less restricted in their access to the outdoors gain competence in moving through the larger world. Developmentally, they gain the ability to navigate their immediate environs (in safety) and lay the foundation for the courage that will enable them eventually to lead their own lives.

When we deprive our children of the opportunity to soar through the sky on a swing and feel as though they were flying, or to hang from their legs on the trapeze as though they were above the crowd in a circus tent, we are actually robbing them of their ability to dream! Stopping them from forming a baseball, basketball, or tag game without "appropriate" adult intervention denies them an experience of spontaneously teaming with and believing in their playmates. If we prohibit our children from engaging in "risky" activities—from conquering a jungle gym to maneuvering an overhead ladder—how will they ever develop their ability to "dare"? And if we fail to encourage them to experience the joy of accomplishment from building a castle or village in the sandbox, how will they learn solid planning and "doing" skills? Fun and play are imperative to strengthening one's imagination, creative abilities, and most of all, innovative thinking.

Lest you believe that play and fun are nonessential ingredients to leading a healthy and productive adult life, consider the following: a robust laugh will burn up to 3.5 calories; a preschooler laughs four hundred times a day, whereas an average thirty-five-year-old only fifteen times a day; laughing releases endorphins, opioid proteins with about ten times the pain-relieving power of morphine; play increases creative thinking; and fun relieves boredom and fatigue, and also improves communication!

So why is it that fun is a "four-letter word" in most companies? The reason is that most of them are run by SOPs (that's SOPs—standard operating procedures), and fun is not part of this ubiquitous ritual. Also, there's an overabundance of corporate "fun squelchers" who fear disruption and disorder, which in their myopic view, equates to a dreaded loss of productivity. Yet the level of fun and play in an organization has a direct influence on morale—the best prescription for a company to run at peak performance. Pixar director Brad Bird (*The Incredibles, Ratatouille*) has said, "The most significant impact on a movie's budget—but never in the budget—is morale. If you have low morale, for every one dollar you spend, you get about twenty-five cents of value. If you have high morale, for every dollar you spend you get about three dollars of value. Companies should pay much more attention to morale." George Zimmer, CEO and founder of Men's Wearhouse, told us, "Most businesses repress our natural tendency to have fun and to socialize. The idea seems that in order to succeed, you have to suffer. But I believe you do your best work when you are feeling enthusiastic about things." Just remember this: one of the best side effects of encouraging fun at work is that it inspires employees to think outside the box and be more innovative—and that's certainly not a waste of time or energy! Most important, can we afford to let our most cherished resource—our employees—feel stifled, unappreciated, and burned out?

Play is serious! Go to any school playground and watch five- and six-year-olds at play. Observe the creativity, tenacity, focus, determination, and perseverance they possess. In his 1938 book *Homo Ludens*, Dutch cultural historian Johan Huizinga lends credence to the power of play, describing it as the primary formative element in human culture. According to Huizinga, "The play-mode is one of rapture and enthusiasm. . . . A feeling of exaltation and tension accompanies the action."

We absolutely love his words describing meaningful play: *rapture*—jubilation, passion, satisfaction; *enthusiasm*—energy, frenzy, zest; *exaltation*—euphoria, grandeur, magnification. Meaningful innovation *requires* meaningful play.

How playful is your organization?

- Is it common to hear laughter coming from your employees?
- Does the laughter stop or diminish when management is around?
- Is the workplace humor good-natured constructive ribbing rather than destructive sarcastic criticism?
- Does your boss usually have an optimistic and happy attitude?
- When something gets screwed up, can team members step back and laugh at their mistake?
- Do you have fun celebrations on a regular basis?
- Is the physical workplace conducive to fun?

◆ Do you engage your customers (internal or external) in your fun environment?

If you answered "no" to two or more of these questions, your organization may be suffering from terminal "sobriety flippancy" (abstinence from humor).

The average employee works 40 hours a week, or 1,920 hours a year (excluding vacation and holidays) or 86,400 hours in an average work life. This accounts for more than *one-third* of his or her waking hours. Life is simply too short not to enjoy your work. One of our clients told us, "I don't always like my job when I go home at night, but I am always energized in the morning to get back to work."

Here are seven actions to fire up your workplace:

1. Create a unique playground. Upon entering Pixar's football stadium-sized atrium, you might think to yourself, "What a waste of space!" But Steve Jobs's vision was to design a building where people would interact naturally. Steve positioned the mailboxes, meeting rooms, cafeteria, and most important, the bathrooms in the center atrium. He realized that when people casually interact and have fun, good things happen and constructive ideas are exchanged. So rather than going off to the software coding, animation, or production departments and spending the entire day there with little or no interaction with folks from other areas of the organization, it is nearly impossible not to run into employees from other departments throughout the course of a day.

Décor also contributes to a playful, fun atmosphere. The atrium at Pixar is decorated with larger-than-life statues of Pixar characters and concept paintings on the walls, with storyboards and color scripts in clear view. Pixar's rolling, sixteen-acre campus also includes offices, studio and sound rooms, screening rooms, a lap pool, volleyball courts, and a soccer field (which is being sacrificed for a new four-level building to provide expanded work/play space)—all of which make for a welcomed escape from the daily grind. As Pixar artist Nate Wragg told us, "It's the freedom and encouragement to relax between deadlines and to take fun breaks when you are feeling tired that I feel really creates that fun atmosphere at work that most businesses lack."

What if you are a struggling company that doesn't have the financial resources to allocate to grand entry halls and swimming pools? Prior to the success of *Toy Story,* Pixar Studios was housed in what Ed Catmull referred to as a "scrappy" cluster of buildings in Point Richmond, California. The company couldn't afford to purchase theater seats for the animation screening room, so John Lasseter set his creative wheels in motion. Inspired by the counterculture hippie décor of the Red Vic Movie Theater in San Francisco's Haight-Ashbury district, John enlisted company-wide support to scout for hand-me-down furniture and, on his own time, drove around in a rented truck to retrieve the discards. When all was said and done, John commented that Pixar now had "the most ugly collection of '70s couches you've ever seen" and that the "room became kind of the soul of Pixar."

Isn't that what any organization needs to discover— what drives an individual's creative spirit? It doesn't have to be an extravagantly decorated room or a collection of costly "stuff"; it just has to be what employees feel represents who they really are.

When Pixar first moved into their glitzy new Emeryville studios, there was some remorse about leaving the "old" Point Richmond habitat. Director Lee Unkrich (*Toy Story 3*) commented, "When we first moved in, there was some concern that the place wasn't us— that it was somehow too nice for us." Lasseter remembers telling Steve Jobs, "You can make an elegantly cool minimalist design, but as soon as the animators are in there, they're going to be pounding up old garbage cans they got for 80 percent off at Kmart." One might think John has a crystal ball among his many office toys, since he seemed to predict that one: A local Kmart store did hold a going-out-of-business, 90 percent off sale just after the move was completed. Pixarians had a field day! Lee revealed, "The moment that the animators started bringing their stuff in and making the offices their own, it was pretty clear that things weren't going to change that much."

Even though Steve Jobs initially had a lack of enthusiasm for the animators' wacky decorations, he came to realize that "if you came up to our new building and said, 'This is the best corporate headquarters in the world,' we would have failed. The new studio had to be a *home*, not a headquarters."

If you want to be innovative, make the workplace a home-away-from-home, and remember you will spend one-third of your life there!

2. Think play! Each month, assign a "recess team" to dream up a fun experience (see "Forty-One Neat Things to Unleash Your Imagination," for ideas). A favorite example of ours is Pixar's scooter races. One day, John Lasseter brought his son's scooter into work and began riding it around. Soon other employees showed up with scooters—and before long, there was a small fleet of them. Director Pete Docter said, "We got into these scooter races—there was a track mapped out, kind of a loop, and we'd time people and write the times on the wall. We all got into a very fierce competition over who could get the best time." Today, the "scooter tradition" is still alive at Pixar; it's commonplace to see someone buzzing by on a scooter.

3. Allow personalized work spaces. Encourage employees to demonstrate their creativity by decorating their individual offices, cubicles, desks, or work areas. Pixar's animation department has the most fabulously decked-out work space one could imagine—a tiki hut, a pagoda bunk bed, and a parachute covering a line of cubicles that resembles a circus tent. Just about any wacky, wild, or interesting structure that you can imagine has eventually found its way into the house of Pixar: a saloon, a 1960s den, a U-shaped restaurant booth, a barber's chair, a pair of hair-dryer chairs from a beauty salon. There's also a plethora of quips and quotes spattering the offices of employees. One of the animators has this phrase of Ed Catmull's tacked to his office door: "Every time you think something stupid's going on, it probably is." Just remember that allowing people to create their own unique statement of individuality goes a long way in fostering an environment of mutual respect and trust.

4. Celebrate! Make time for celebrations to note life's milestones—a birthday, an anniversary, a graduation. Make time to pull out all the stops and showcase the talents and accomplishments of an entire team. Whenever a new Pixar feature film is released, they stage a release celebration—a black-tie luncheon event where the employees don their finest to commemorate the film's completion and celebrate another dream come true. Your celebrations don't have to be on par with the grand Pixar style of ceremonial hoopla. Just giving people a reason to get out of their offices to celebrate and connect with others in a unique and special way can do wonders for their morale.

5. Grant employees permission to be recognized for their work by "outsiders." Encourage employees to join professional associations in which they have an opportunity to display their work, gain peer and industry recognition for their accomplishments, and most of all, have fun. Pixar's cofounder Alvy Ray Smith told us, "A lot of companies keep everything absolutely secret. We understood one of the reasons that we had some of the hottest talent in the business was not only because it was glamorous but because we let these people get their form of glory. To publish in academic journals and get their fame—that's more important to our kind of people than money." Former Pixar employee Lou Romano shared with us that he believes working on artwork and projects outside the studio is "probably the single most important element that keeps people creative and productive in the workplace."

6. Be a role model for mutual respect and trust. The level of mutual respect and trust in your workplace is directly proportional to workers' attitudes regarding play and fun. When the workplace is dominated by fear, emotions of disdain, animosity, and apathy can thrive and grow—all of which are counterproductive to creating a playful, fun environment. *Fish!*—the story of Pike Place Fish Market in Seattle, Washington—is one of the most successful accounts of fun in the workplace. Our friend John Christensen, coauthor of *Fish!* (who also penned the foreword for our revised edition of *The Disney Way*), maintains that you simply cannot duplicate what the fishmongers do on the shores of the Pacific Ocean. John says, "If you don't have the shared commitment and trust that make playfulness possible at work, it may not happen." We have witnessed a company director attempting to mandate fun, and behind his back, employees referred to it as "FFT"—"forced fun time." Innovative thinkers resent being forced to have fun—and for that matter, anything else. Certainly, fun and play are not tools to be taken out of the drawer once a month. They are attitudes that must be embraced, and without the underlying component of mutual respect and trust, they can never become internalized in any culture.

7. Laugh at yourself. Leaders who demonstrate self-deprecating humor set the tone for workplace play and fun. Why is joking and not taking yourself too seriously important for leaders? Leaders need to be seen as authentic human beings—which leads us back, once again, to the values of mutual respect and trust. When leaders take themselves too seriously, they create a barrier, an emotional distance that fosters feelings of distrust within employees. Leadership requires an emotional connection and cannot be facilitated by rigidity, fear, and intimidation.

When you take yourself too seriously,

life ceases to be fun.

A recent national Gallup study identified three types of employees: "engaged," "not-engaged," and "disengaged." Engaged employees are those who feel happy and passionate about their jobs and who have a profound connection to the company. They drive innovation. Not-engaged employ-

ees are those who have "checked out" and seem to sleep-
walk through the day, putting in their time without energy
or passion. Finally, the disengaged employees are those who
are unhappy and who openly display their unhappiness.

The good news is that Gallup survey research indicates
that "engaged employees are more productive, profitable,
safer, create stronger customer relationships, and stay
longer with their company than less engaged employees"
and that "workplace engagement is also a powerful factor in catalyzing 'outside-the-box' thinking to improve
management and business processes as well as customer
service." The bad news is that among the entire sample of
1,000 employees, only 29 percent considered themselves
"engaged"; 56 percent responded "not-engaged," and 15
percent responded "actively disengaged."

Leaders must step forward and set the tone of the organization by encouraging a time for play or recess. Let's
recap the benefits of meaningful play cited by the Association of Education for Young Children—and yes, these
benefits also apply to the "adult" workplace!

- Unite mind, body, and spirit
- Reduce tension
- Express and work out emotional issues
- Develop objectivity, seeing things through another
  person's point of view—cooperating, helping, shar-
  ing, and solving problems
- Enhance ones' perceptual abilities that suffer when so
  much of their experience is through television, com-

puters, books, worksheets, and media that require
only two senses

♦ Inspire courage to take appropriate risks

Here is Pixar director Andrew Stanton's advice for pre-
venting emotional exhaustion: "Laugh hard, twice daily."
He said, "Something is terribly wrong if I don't crack up at
least a couple times a day."

Time for recess—let's play!

Bill and Lynn's Chalkboard

The team that plays together
stays together . . . and
exciting things happen!

10

Forty-One Neat Things to Unleash Your Imagination

JOHN LASSETER BELIEVES that creative ideas can come from anywhere. As Pete Docter explained, "I think John's a really great example. . . . He can see the potential in everything that's offered to him. . . . I think that has rippled down and become a big part of what makes Pixar a good place. There's just an energizing joy of life, a receptiveness to inspiration from anything and anyone and anywhere."

Here are forty-one neat things that we believe will help your company or team to improve its innovative process:

1. Take a road trip. In preparation for the animated feature film *Cars,* Lasseter contacted Route 66 historian Michael Wallis. Lasseter, Wallis, and eleven animators rented white Cadillacs and traveled Route 66. David Overton, cofounder of The Cheesecake Factory, frequently takes "tasting road trips" with his team. The team will have three lunches and three dinners *each day.* Take a road trip with your team to get some hands-on experience with your product or service.

2. Collect artifacts that inspire good work. During the *Cars* road trips, Lasseter and his team collected items they found along the roadside—hub caps, wheat, snake skins, and even roadkill. A consultant friend of Bill's keeps an artifact from each of his clients and displays these items in his office. We have a collection of Walt Disney photos and artwork in our office. What artifacts would inspire your team?

3. Go fact finding. To obtain ideas for designing the *Cars* movie characters, Lasseter visited the actual design studios of several automotive companies. Over the years, we have assisted scores of clients in taking various types of field trips. They have visited suppliers to learn how to serve one another more effectively, visited Walt Disney World to experience world-class customer service, or visited retail outlets to hear potential customer comments and observe customer reactions to their products. Consider field trips that seem completely disconnected. Visit a clothing store when looking for a new design for tractors, Menard's Hardware when designing a new clothing line for kids or women, a farm supply store for ideas on how to improve iPods. Be incongruous! What field trips would expand your team's imagination?

4. Go to the park and play. Plan an afternoon outing for your team to play together at a local park—swing, play tag, organize a kick ball game, and so on. After a couple of hours, take a refreshment break and debrief the afternoon. How did it feel to play like a little kid again? How did that feeling compare to your day-to-day feelings about your work? How can we capture that childlike enthusiasm in our work life?

5. Go to an art museum. Take your team to a museum for the day. Break the team into small groups of two or three people and assign each group a different art genre—abstract, contemporary, impressionists, surrealism, and so forth. Have each group prepare its thoughts on how that style of art could complement or enhance your product or service. At the end of the day or the next morning, share ideas with the whole team.

6. Encourage individual creative work spaces. Pixar's animation department looks a lot like the Munchkin set for *The Wizard of Oz*. The animators wanted work spaces different from the typical cookie-cutter corporate cubicles. Pixar found little cottages, and each animator decorated a cottage/office as he or she saw fit. Encourage work space creativity—have a "most creative work space of the month" contest.

7. Visit your local fire department. Remember when you were in first grade and your class took a field trip to the local firehouse? Take your team to the firehouse, and interview the chief and his team. Ask how standard procedures and creativity are used together to fight a fire. The next day, discuss how this might apply to your creative process. What things always need to be done "by the book" and what things need to be constantly challenged, changed, and improved?

8. Open a dream room. Designate an office or small conference room as a dream room. Post creative ideas on storyboards around the room. Encourage everyone to stop by the room at least once a week to add ideas and comments to the existing storyboards or to start a new one. Include photos, magnetic words, and felt characters on the "idea storyboard." Post all idea storyboards on the company intranet.

9. Declare a "Do Nothing, No Tech" day. Every so often your creative team needs to recharge its batteries. For one full day, cancel all meetings, take only critical phone calls, and insist on no use of Blackberry, e-mail, or other technology. Spend the day reading, daydreaming, writing, or drawing by hand. Recharge your batteries.

10. Take quiet time. Designate one hour each day for quiet time. That means no meetings, phone calls, e-mail, or text messaging, just quiet, thinking, and planning time.

11. Product marketing teams: don't forget your first name. Too many marketing teams concentrate the majority of their creative efforts on communication and advertising—forgetting that their "first name" is *Product!* Walk in your customers' shoes. If you are trying to create a new service for your customers, go out in the marketplace and participate as a customer. If you are designing a new product, use the competition's product to find out what you like and don't like. Each month Frank Lloyd Wright, one of the premiere architects of all time, had his students take turns preparing a formal dinner for fellow classmates. Wright felt that too many architects never prepared anything in the kitchen and had no idea of how the design of a kitchen either helped or hindered the complexity of dinner preparation. Use your product. Observe others using your product.

12. Establish a "Jr. brain trust." Select a group of children ages seven to twelve to act as advisors to your team. Looking at your problems through a child's eyes can be enlightening. There's a story about a tall truck that while trying to pass through the Holland Tunnel in New York City got wedged inside the entrance. Engineers and other experts debated for hours the best way to remove the truck with minimal damage. Of course, traffic was backed up for miles. Then, after observing the situation from the window of a nearby car, a little girl apparently said to one of the engineers, "Hey, mister, why don't you just let the air out of the tires?" Leonardo da Vinci was right when he realized that "simplicity is the ultimate sophistication." Get a fresh perspective—a child's perspective may be just what you need.

13. Establish a "Sr. brain trust." By 2015, more than 25 percent of the U.S. population will be age sixty-five or older, and by 2025, almost 30 percent. Just like children, seniors will give you a new and different perspective on your creative journey.

14. Celebrate the failure of the month. Unfortunately, most failed projects follow these six phases: 1. enthusiasm; 2. disillusionment; 3. panic; 4. search for the guilty; 5. punishment of the innocent; 6. praise and honors for nonparticipants. Innovative companies and teams learn from their mistakes. Pixar has developed a postmortem process that is used for all projects. (And at the time of this writing, they have yet to release an unsuccessful feature film.) Start a "Screw-up of the Month Award" and learn from your mistakes. This award will highlight the benefits of learning from mistakes; it is not a punishment.

15. Bring in an outside guest speaker. Have your team spend an afternoon learning how to cultivate bonsai trees, or how to prepare an Italian dinner, or how to make classical music relevant to today's youth. Hire your local arts council staff for an "art attack"—a company onsite art/creativity lesson. The key is to get the team to expand their thinking outside their "normal" comfort thinking zone.

16. Stretch the limits of the comfort zone. Arrange a karaoke night. Plan a team dinner, but don't say anything about the karaoke. Before dinner, form subteams of four or five members. Give the teams a prearranged list of songs and ask them to select one that best describes their team. At dinner, ask the teams to explain why they chose their songs. After the first team presents their explanation, unveil the karaoke equipment and ask them to perform the song. When all the subteams have performed, continue with traditional karaoke. You will be amazed to see the barriers break down within a team. Use your imagination to arrange other comfort zone stretching activities. Some other suggestions include bumper cars, an obstacle course, various low ropes outdoor activities, and handicap awareness trails.

17. Give your project or team a cool name. How can you expect a team to be creative if they are members of the "accounts receivable process improvement team"? Boring. How about the "get the piggy (bank) to market quicker team"? Have one of the team member's kids draw a mascot to represent your new team name. Change the drawing every month to give other kids an opportunity to draw a mascot. Make it exciting and fun.

18. Give all team members an NTHR (Neat Things Happening Recorder). For less than fifty dollars you can purchase a digital voice recorder about the size of a pack of gum. Ask team members to get into the habit of recording neat experiences outside of work on an NTHR. Maybe an idea will come to them at the local hardware store, at a rock concert or other musical performance, or at their daughter's school open house. Remember what John Lasseter said about inspiration coming "from anything and anyone and anywhere." Be prepared to capture the inspiration with your NTHR.

19. Don't let the ankle biters get you. Have you ever had one of those tiny little dogs that is no higher than your ankle come nipping at you? If you completely ignore them, they usually go away without causing any damage since their mouths are too small to fit around your ankle. But if you stop and bend over and try to calm them down, you could loose a finger. Workplace ankle biters are no different. They are the perpetual naysayers—"That will never work," or "We can't afford to try this," or "Management will never approve." Don't let them get to you! If you bend down to their level, they will destroy your team's momentum, creativity, and attitude. Ignore the naysayers!

20. Ask "What if?" and "Why not?" Walt Disney said, "It's fun doing the impossible." Encourage your team to dream about doing the impossible and to constantly challenge conventional wisdom.

21. Get everyone in the "sandbox"—all for one and one for all! Part-time team members can destroy the team's attitude and creativity. If your team needs critical creative input from marketing, purchasing, accounting, or any other "specialty function," try to budget for their full-time commitment. If your budget can't handle the added expense, get creative. Maybe the person from purchasing can track the budget, or perhaps the marketing guru can coordinate subcontractors. What's important is to have full-time members who are first and foremost committed to the successful team outcome, not their individual department objectives.

22. Do something audacious every day. It becomes very easy to get stuck in a rut doing the same old thing day after day. Do something recklessly bold every single day—write your weekly sales report in crayon, have a pint of ice cream for lunch, wear your pajamas to work, have a tea party for your team where everyone wears white gloves—the point is not to get into a rut. Be lively, unrestrained, and uninhibited!

23. Embrace chaos and confusion. Don't wait for all the answers. Innovation by its very definition requires a level of uncertainty. Try, fail, learn, and try again. If you get it right the first time, it's probably not very innovative.

24. Hire someone who is your complete opposite. Creativity requires diversity of ideas. We have helped scores of clients implement the Myers-Briggs Type Indicator and behavioral styles instruments for team members to understand their unique gifts. Different is good.

25. Share. Share successes, failures, experiences, and ideas. They can be catalysts that propel your innovative culture. Share these successes often and not just at weekly or monthly staff meetings.

26. Do "smart" benchmarking. "Dumb" benchmarking is spending one year studying your industry's leader, and three years trying to be just like them. In the meantime, the leader is off doing something even more remarkable. "Smart" benchmarking is seeing what you can learn from someone totally outside your industry. For example, if you are a plumbing contractor, what can you learn from the Four Seasons Hotels and Resorts, Disney, or Starbucks? Innovate, don't imitate!

27. Get engaging. Engage—connect, interest, involve, immerse, hang out, join, mesh—with other departments, vendors, customers (current, lost, angry, potential), and frontline employees (the best source of "wow" ideas). Get out of your office or department and listen to exhilarating ideas. Engaging People = Cool Innovations. Nonengaging People = Dull Innovations.

28. Innovation begins in human resources. An innovative culture is a more important factor in the human resources department than in the engineering, new product development, or marketing departments. Think about it: if HR only hires dull people, only creates hard skills training programs, and conducts policy-driven orientation sessions, the result will be a dull and unimaginative culture. Exciting people and stimulating training are "musts" for an inspiring, innovative culture.

29. Celebrate everything. Commemorate milestones, birthdays, "grand" failures, tremendous successes—Fridays, Wednesdays, Mondays. Celebrations = Fun = People Enjoying Each Other = Innovative Culture.

30. "Bam! Kick it up a notch." Do like Chef Emeril Lagasse says and "kick it up a notch." "Bam!" These are two of his favorite catchphrases usually said right before or after adding more spice to one of his culinary creations to make it more interesting or exciting. When you think something is good enough—Bam it, kick it up a notch, raise the bar!

31. Partner with academia. Research universities are critical to ongoing innovation. Establish small or large, formal or informal partnerships.

32. Cross-functional innovation teams rock. Over the years, we have witnessed that the success of innovation is directly proportional to the cross-functionality of a team. Often, the over-the-top innovative ideas come from support team members rather than operational team members.

33. Create a subsidiary organization for innovation. When companies succeed and get large, they often lose agility and get complacent. What once was the remarkable breakthrough is now taken for granted—they own the market, and the need to innovate is lost until another company creates the next new remarkable product. Remember Sony? They once owned the portable music market. In the 1980s and 1990s, a "Walkman" meant a portable music device, and Walkmans were practically everywhere. Then in 2001, the iPod redefined the market. Create a subsidiary organization for innovation with its own staffing and culture to avoid becoming complacent. Walt Disney did this with his WED (Walter Elias Disney) Enterprise in 1952 to develop his theme park. And in a way, Pixar has continued to operate as a subsidiary-type culture within the walls of its giant parent, The Walt Disney Company.

34. Decentralize. Smaller, enabled, and trusted decentralized units become closer to the customer—the resulting workforce is more intimate, and the commitment to innovation is easier to cultivate. In May 2009, Pixar announced that it will open a studio in Vancouver, British Columbia, to produce mainly short-form quality computer animation. Once your organization grows larger than five hundred employees, consider decentralizing. Don't just "kinda" decentralize by allowing production and sales to be independent but prohibiting field operations from trying out wacky new product or service ideas. Beware of the corporate headquarters corner office control freaks that decentralize in name only.

35. Support innovation in your local school system. Children are your future workforce. The educational system should foster innovation, not stifle it. Get involved. Host storyboarding sessions in local schools and then donate a portion of the profit from the new product or service you create. Make the kids and the school your innovation partners. How many cool new products or experiences can your school create? Make a difference.

36. Conduct quarterly "Gong Shows." Years ago, the Disney organization had something called the "Gong Show." This was an opportunity for anyone in the company to pitch new film ideas. Launch your own "Gong Show."

37. Make everyone an innovator. Walt Disney believed that everyone is creative. We all may not be able to come up with the next iPod, Blackberry, or microchip, but almost everyone sees innovative opportunities in the way they conduct their jobs or serve their customers. Encourage, reward, and trust employees to be innovative in how they do their jobs. The results will surprise you.

38. Solve problems, don't just make better products. In the late 1990s, the problem with the portable CD player was the need to lug around and care for a large number of rather fragile CDs. Apple came in and solved the problem with the iPod. The problem with the traditional circus was caring for the wild animals and affording as well as attracting well-known circus performers. Enter Cirque du Soleil. They reinvented the circus experience without big-name performers or wild animals. Think "problem solving," not "product redesign."

39. Ask innovative questions—what, who, how, and where? What value is being added by the problem you are solving? Who is the customer? How will you make your product? Where are the markets and distribution channels for the new product or service?

40. Mentor innovators. Ask your most seasoned and innovative free-thinking employees to mentor new hires. Engage in open discussion with new hires to discover their initial impressions of your culture. If they do not feel, sense, or identify a true passion for innovation, something needs to be done to improve the culture. Until that total unwavering passionate commitment to an innovative culture is felt by all, especially new hires, your results will be less than desirable. Use mentoring to solidify and test the spirit of innovation in your organization.

41. Establish a department of intrapreneurism. This department must be a team of internal venture capitalists. Allow employees to present rip-roaring ideas and business plans for startup consideration. Remember to reward big successes and excellent failures (quick, good tries and solid lessons learned).

Exciting Imaginative Culture	Dull Unimaginative Culture
Linked employees	Ranked employees
Seek ideas through collaboration	Top-down ideas
Enabling others = power	Telling others = power
Teach soft and hard skills	Teach only hard skills
Live with ambiguity	Pragmatic facts only
Make intuitive decisions	Rational decisions only
Flexible, quick to act	Inflexible, slow to act
Become highly diversified	Little diversity
Make work play	Work requires suffering

Will your company create products and experiences as innovative as Walt Disney's animated feature film art form, Steve Jobs's iPod, Pixar's computer-generated film process, and Cirque du Soleil's new circus experience? Or will you stick with old products like vinyl records, cassette tapes, or VCR tape players? Turn vinyl records into placemats, jewelry, ornaments, or magnets; use VCR tape to wrap the boss's car or make wigs for all employees; build a playhouse from old cassettes and vinyl records to create "the ultimate entertainment center."

"We worked really hard, but we also had so much fun, and it showed up in our work. We'd goof off, we'd laugh, we'd work together, and we'd look at and give feedback on each other's stuff. And the creativity just sort of overflowed."

—John Lasseter

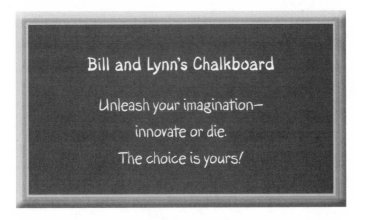

Bill and Lynn's Chalkboard

Unleash your imagination—
innovate or die.
The choice is yours!

DO UNLEASH YOUR CHILDLIKE POTENTIAL

Do really **good work** and really **good things** happen.

There is no **right way** to do the **wrong thing.**

Quality is the best business plan!

All for one, and one for **all.**

Always do the **best** you can!

DO!

BUT HOW WILL WE MAXIMIZE QUARTERLY PROFITS?

IF IT MAKES MONEY IT'S GOOD ENOUGH!

FOLLOW THE STANDARD PROCEDURE!!

FLICK

SECTION 4

11

How Do You
Measure a Dream?

"DO NOT COLOR outside the lines." "Do this. Don't do that." "That's correct." "That's not the way I showed you." "Here's what your paper should look like." Yes, there are rigid standards of performance that adults use to both measure and evaluate our work. We learn this very early in life. (Believe it or not, some schools actually *grade* kindergarten students on how well they color inside the lines.) Distinguished music educator Carroll Rinehart, a member of the original design team for OMA (Opening Minds Through the Arts), explained that this practice is prevalent even in fine arts education: "Part of the problem we are facing in this country is that some of the models are very restrictive. You can go almost anyplace and see the exact same lesson replicated, and that's not what art is about." In the first few years of grade school, it seems that we are told what creativity is and what it's not. When Walt Disney was a young schoolboy, he was once asked to draw flowers in art class. Walt embellished his flowers by sketching a face in the center of each one. The teacher was less than impressed by his deviation from the norm. Fortunately for us, however, she failed to stifle this creative genius whose dream world would go on to make him one of the most famous artists in history.

Certainly, school would be a lot more exciting if we didn't have to worry about grades and report cards or being labeled a "talker" or a "daydreamer" or "ADD/ADHD." The whole educational system can be a huge distraction from our freedom to learn and discover what we love doing, what we are good at, and most important, simply how to be the best we can be.

At the end of formal schooling, as we begin our professional journey to success, we are faced with some of the same performance standards as before—"do this," "don't do that"—but there's more. Concepts like "measuring productivity gains" and "cost-benefit analysis" now relate directly to how our work affects the company's bottom line. For decades, the corporate world has been obsessed with measurements as the primary metric of success. Many of these arbitrary efficiency metrics are destroying the creativity, innovation, and morale of today's workplace. As early as 1980, Dr. W. Edwards Deming, father of the Total Quality Management movement and authority on modern management practices, is often incorrectly quoted as saying, "You can't manage what you can't measure." In fact, Deming warned about "running a company on visible figures alone"—one of what he called "the Seven Deadly Diseases" of management. In his book *Out of the Crisis* (1989), Dr. Deming states, "The most important figures that one needs for management are unknown or unknowable, but successful management must nevertheless take account of them."

The sad fact is that in too many companies, frontline employees take the heat for poor results that are due to careless or ill-informed leadership. The employees are subject to ineffective systems and processes, resulting in negative performance appraisals. "Guilty until proven innocent" seems to be the operating judicial code. This is tragic because employees are all too often the victims, not the perpetrators, of workplace dysfunction. They are battered by forces beyond their control. This practice is demonstrated by Dr. Deming's infamous "Bead Factory" exercise. In this exercise, workers are told the white beads are a good quality product, and the red beads are a bad quality product. They are given a paddle to scoop out beads from a container of red and white beads using only one hand. Approximately 20 percent of the beads in the container are red, but the workers are told that "zero defects" is their goal. Workers are evaluated based on their outputs even though the results are due entirely to chance. The number of defective red beads is a result of the process, not the worker. Enlightened leadership should use measurement to determine process capability. They must learn to attack the process, not the people. (For detailed instructions on conducting the "Red Bead Factory" exercise, see *The Disney Way Fieldbook,* scene 36.)

The point is that in too many organizations, the fixation on short-term results causes management to focus on unrealistic production standards resulting in a demoralized workforce, often causing further declines in productivity. After *Toy Story*'s phenomenal success in 1995, Steve Jobs decided that taking Pixar public would be in the best long-term interests of the company. But Ed Catmull and John Lasseter were deeply concerned that Wall Street's short-term—"red bead"—mentality would dramatically change the innovative culture that they worked so hard to establish. John remembers telling Steve, "The day that happened would be the day I left the company." He continued, "Steve looked at me and said, 'I will never ask you to do that.' So we made a kind of a deal. It was a simple philosophy—just keep making the films, have fun doing it, and don't worry about the latest stock price."

McKinsey & Company director Lowell L. Bryan advises companies to focus on measuring the "intangible" contributions of their people and says "the most valuable capital that companies possess today is precisely intangible rather than financial." Pixar's deeply held leadership values that focus on mutual respect for all employees and the quality of their art form have contributed to their skyrocketing financial and artistic success. And, let's give credit where credit is due: Disney CEO Bob Iger deserves credit for promising Pixar the autonomy that fosters unbridled creativity. Under Bob, Pixar employees aren't pressured to take different roads simply to chase profits and compromise their desire to remain true to who they are. Entertainment specialist Doug Creutz, vice president of Cowen and Company Investment Bankers, commented in April of 2009, "The worries keep coming, despite Pixar's track record, because each film it delivers seems to be less commercial than the last." Bob Iger's response to this comment was, "We seek to make great films first. If the film gives birth to a franchise, we are the first company to leverage such success. A check-the-boxes approach to creativity is likely to result in blandness and failure."

Three cheers for Iger! He really gets it: make great films and the bottom line will follow!

Pixar's band of self-motivated talent is always in a "want to" mode— enthusiastically improving on everything they do. Their cheerleader, Mr. Creativity himself, John Lasseter, has a passion for excellence that is reflected in those all-too-

often overlooked intangible cultural measures that keep
the Pixar "band" playing—employee loyalty, freedom, collaboration, and the list goes on and on. These might be an
off-the-charts "lightning in a bottle" fuzzy measurement,
but the tangible results speak volumes.

Consider this stick of financial measurement:

Pixar's Box-Office Results (in Thousands)

Release Date	Movie Name	1st Weekend	U.S. Gross	Worldwide Gross	Budget
11/22/1995	Toy Story	$29,140	$191,796	$361,996	$30,000
11/20/1998	A Bug's Life	$291	$162,798	$363,398	$45,000
11/19/1999	Toy Story 2	$300	$245,852	$485,752	$90,000
11/2/2001	Monsters, Inc.	$62,577	$255,870	$528,970	$115,000
5/30/2003	Finding Nemo	$70,251	$339,714	$866,592	$94,000
11/5/2004	The Incredibles	$70,467	$261,441	$635,564	$92,000
6/9/2006	Cars	$60,119	$244,082	$461,982	$70,000
6/29/2007	Ratatouille	$47,027	$206,445	$624,445	$150,000
6/27/2008	WALL-E	$63,087	$223,806	$532,936	$180,000
5/29/2009	Up	$68,200	—	—	$175,000
Totals			$2,131,804	$4,861,635	$1,041,000
Averages			$236,867	$540,182	$104,100

Source: Box-office data courtesy Nash Information Services, LLC
(www.the-numbers.com).

Just "managing by the numbers" one could take heed of Creutz's concern that each Pixar film since *Finding Nemo* (2003) has been less of a commercial success. (*WALL-E* grossed only 3 times its budget, compared to *Nemo,* which grossed 9.2 times its budget.) Each has been an overwhelming *critical* success, however, and it is hard to say what the long-term commercial success of these films will be. For example, *Snow White* grossed $66.6 million when released in 1937, and through 1977 it grossed $184.9 million in rereleases to theaters and tens of millions more in video and DVD releases ($74 million alone in 2001). In 1940, *Pinocchio* lost money, grossing only $1.9 million and costing $2.6 million to produce, yet like *Snow White* through 1977, *Pinocchio*'s rereleases to theaters have grossed $84.3 million, and in its first week of release the seventieth anniversary Platinum Edition DVD sold $23.8 million.

The point is, as John Lasseter stated, "Quality is the best business plan." Many historical film critics consider *Pinocchio* to be the best animated feature film ever produced. Yet if someone like Creutz had convinced Walt in 1940 that he needed to manage by just short-term measurements and produce "more commercial" films, we might have had a string of unoriginal, trite, dull, and predictable *Snow White II, III,* and *IV* films, rather than *Bambi* (1942), *Cinderella* (1950), and *Peter Pan* (1953). Good was just not good enough for Walt. The quality of his films had to possess a hellacious mastery surpassing the audience's wildest expectations. His films have transcended the ages, captivating as many as seven generations of youngsters, and will more than likely captivate another seven generations.

Pixar, like Walt, is in perpetual motion, always exploring the world through a child's eyes of wonder. Creativity at its best means beginning each new project with a clean slate—not resting on one's laurels of past accomplishments. It's all about chasing a dream that is fresh and exciting—not driven by any formula—leading the company by those most important intangible measurements. And it's the fortitude to stay the course all the way through what Mohammed Ali called "the lonely work"—the part of work where you don't get any kudos, accolades, or rewards. It takes a firm belief that something will turn out wonderful in the end (a four-year "lonely" journey for the typical Pixar film).

So if we shouldn't judge the creative effort by visible figures alone, and the most important figures are unknown, how do we measure innovation in a company?

Any organization's innovative process requires three metrics:

1. Top leadership who is totally enamored with and enchanted by innovation, and who expects the same from everyone in the organization, from the boardroom to the storeroom.

2. Frontline leadership who facilitates and encourages creative ideas from the entire team; a work environment that enables employees to quickly try new and innova-

tive ways of doing their jobs, learn from their experiences, and try again.

3. Tangible measurements that are meaningful to the business process.

Pixar's innovative process meets these criteria in spades—the monumental intangible measures of leadership, quality, and mutual respect; and the tangible budgetary and production metrics. This is how Pixar measures a dream!

Their best is as good as it gets.

But their best is yet to come!

Bill and Lynn's Chalkboard

Managing innovation by
numbers alone will result
in unimaginative and trite
customer experiences!

12

"Let's Make a Dent in the Universe"

—Steve Jobs

THE CONCEPT OF quality is understood by children only in terms of what is real and what is meaningful to them. It's the simple things—a double-dip ice-cream cone, a really cool birthday party, a favorite toy, and certainly, the latest Pixar movie—that delight a child. With *Toy Story*'s release in 1995, Pixar quite simply redefined quality in animated movies.

Disney was definitely thinking about the future after *Toy Story*'s phenomenal success, convincing Pixar that making a sequel would be a smart move. The key was coming up with another great story. Lucky for us, inspiration, John Lasseter style, was in the works. One day, John took a good look at the vast array of "untouchable" toys decorating his office. Many of these museum-quality treasures were gifts from famous people like Tom Hanks, who was the voice of Woody. Not even John's own sons are allowed to play with these toys. John thought to himself, what a great premise—a story about one-of-a-kind, priceless toys that no child is allowed to cuddle, sleep with, or befriend. Along with fellow "brain trust" member Pete Docter, John thought the premise had real possibilities. But, at that point in time, he was consumed by *A Bug's Life*, and Pete was entrenched in the development of *Monsters, Inc.* Not about to shelf an idea that could rekindle the public's love affair with the original movie, they delegated the project to some enthusiastic but novice animation and production staffers.

Excitement surrounding the story premise for *Toy Story 2* was escalating, and Disney quickly upgraded the project from a lower scale, direct-to-video production (not uncommon for sequels) to a full-blown theatrical release. Top executives did not, however, have the same high hopes of success for this film that they had for *A Bug's Life*. So Lasseter and the more seasoned animators were assigned to *A Bugs Life*, and again, a younger, less experienced team was assigned to *Toy Story 2*.

Back in those days, top talent was hard to come by. Big players like Disney and DreamWorks were quick to swoop up anyone who might be the next John Lasseter. In contrast, Pixar was on a bare-bones budget, and hiring new people to meet their project demands was just not viable.

The young *Toy Story 2* animation team began creating a storyboard to visually tell the story panel by panel, like a comic book. Storyboarding helps organize drawings and provides a visual format for sharing story ideas before the expense of producing animation begins. Once the storyboards are completed, the team assembles a story reel by combining these rough drawings with sound—beginning dialogue and temporary music. These first story reels are usually pretty rough—much different from the final product. Story reels typically go through many iterations of improvements before the actual animation process can begin. The young project team in charge of *Toy Story 2* began with a solid initial story idea. But by the time they were to start animation, the story reels had not been improved as expected. Trouble was brewing. The story simply wasn't progressing. And to make matters worse, there was a kind of mutiny going on in the ranks.

Picture this point in the history of the company: *Toy Story* had been Pixar's only major theatrical success, *A Bug's Life* was still in postproduction and publicity planning, and *Toy Story 2* needed to be rescued. The very success or failure of the company was at stake.

Once *A Bug's Life* was completed, a distress signal rang out loudly and clearly, and John Lasseter came rushing in to save the struggling team. John reflected, "Steve Jobs gave me probably the greatest piece of advice. He said, 'In a time of crisis, you don't have time to figure out new people around you. Just bring all the people you know and trust around you.' And that's exactly what I did."

Story development had been an exhausting process for the *Toy Story 2* project team, and it was obvious that this film was a long way from where John wanted it to be. After having been immersed in *A Bug's Life* for so long, he decided to get back into the "feel" of *Toy Story* by watching the original movie again with his family. Awestruck by just how wonderful this film really was, John knew that *Toy Story 2* had to be just as magical.

Disney called the shots for Pixar's production deadlines and refused to budge on the original schedule agreed on for *Toy Story 2*. President Ed Catmull revealed, "Given where the production was at the point, eighteen months would have been an aggressive schedule, but by then we had only eight left to deliver the film." So John gathered up his faithful original "brain trust" members, and together they began to breathe new life into the tired story.

Here they were, together again—the core creative team who had been so instrumental in the success of the original *Toy Story*. John Lasseter and Lee Unkrich (editor of both *Toy Story* and *A Bug's Life*), along with now legendary Pixar "brain trust" members Andrew Stanton, the late Joe Ranft, and Pete Docter, found themselves totally jazzed with enthusiasm reliving the storytelling passion they had shared on *Toy Story*. They still believed the original *Toy Story 2* plot was solid but also that the absence of a "wow" factor was more than apparent. And at Pixar, mind you, the "wow" really matters! "I used to say for years that story was the most important thing to us," says Catmull. "Then I realized that all the other studios were saying the same thing. They say that and then they go and produce crap. What you say doesn't mean a damn thing. It's what you do that matters." (*Do* is the operative word here!)

After an evening of bantering and laughing and plus-ing each other's ideas, the brain trust came up with something they believed would dazzle their fellow team members. They just couldn't wait to get the whole team together in the animation pit and get things sailing along again—this time with all hands on deck charting a steady course to victory. And what a sweet victory it was. Released in late November 1999, *Toy Story 2*, Pixar's first theatrical sequel, went on to earn $120 million more than the original movie. Some say the sequel did the impossible—actually improving on the near-perfect original.

So you may be thinking, what about all that "try, learn, and try again" stuff or the corporate babble about the "brain trust" being there to advise, not dictate? When you look closely at the situation, Ed Catmull did allow the initial *Toy Story 2* team to "try, learn, and try again." Some may argue that he did not step in soon enough to "dictate" the change in leadership. But it's difficult to fault his timing—especially when this visionary leader has had such an amazing track record of success. As Ed has said, "Management's job is not to prevent risk but to build the capability to recover when failure occurs."

There are two lessons to be learned from the making of *Toy Story 2*. First, as Lasseter has stated on numerous occasions, "Quality is the best business plan." It makes no difference if you are making a movie that takes four years or serving a customer that takes four minutes, you have only one chance to deliver that magical, magnetic, enchanting experience for your customer. Six months into the production of *Pinocchio*, Walt Disney halted work on the project. His team of animators was about halfway through the meticulous, time-consuming drawings when Walt decided that Pinocchio looked too wooden and Jiminy Cricket looked too much, well, like a cricket. Disney had already won world-wide acclaim and could have allowed the film to be released—probably without any serious damage to the company or its reputation—definitely with substantial savings. But Walt recognized the difference between adequate and excellent. So too did Ed Catmull and John Lasseter. The original *Toy Story* had been such an overwhelming success, and there was every indication that *A Bug's Life* would at least equal that accomplishment. So why did Pixar not take the risk of letting *Toy Story 2* be released with just an average story? It was, after all, just a sequel. Clearly, when it comes to quality, like Walt, Ed and John understand that there is no right way to do the wrong thing.

The second lesson is that it's all about the team—the team is *everything*! As our friend Ken Blanchard, a world-renowned author and speaker, often says, "None of us is as smart as all of us." This may seem overused and cliché, but it's true. We have conducted hundreds of team-building exercises over the years. In one exercise, we present a problem and ask team members to work individually and then as a group to assess the value and prioritize a list of items in terms of their importance to survival. Team answers were substantially better than the average of the individuals' answers in more than 98 percent of cases. In the 2 percent of cases where the average individual answers were better, we were able to identify dysfunctional team behavior—barriers ranging from team members with poor attitudes about their company, to individual or departmental feuds, to gender or racial prejudice.

Pixar is a place where working together works. "Artists and geeks" team up and collaborate. Pixar cofounder Alvy Ray Smith told us, "The artistically creative people like John Lasseter and the animation staff are helpless without the technically creative people. They can't do it, and they know it. So, the only thing that works is to have those two groups of people work hand in hand, almost literally side by side . . . and the only way that can happen is with mutual respect and dignity on all sides. I've never been in another place that had it."

Despite the differences in expertise and experience, Alvy and Ed discovered that there were striking similarities in the temperament of technical staff and animation staff and that, therefore, they must be managed in a similar fashion. Ed explained, "We've got both world-class programmers and world-class artists. Having seen both, I am of the view that there are far fewer differences than most people think. In fact, the more we think about the parallels, the more parallels we see." The groups are in constant communication with one another—scene producers share feedback with animators, and technologists share ideas for new visual effects with directors—all without ever having to worry about being granted permission. The collegiate dynamic between technically and artistically creative folks at Pixar adds a new dimension to John Lasseter's credo: "Technology inspires art, and art challenges the technology." Some years back, Ed and Alvy's collegial organizational structure even piqued the interest of the U.S. Navy—key organizational experts came to Pixar for ideas on improving the navy organization. Pixar's devoted teams continue to lead them to countless awards and nominations, demonstrating that "the whole is definitely greater than the sum of its parts."

We will always choose a quality-driven group of average performers who are committed to a team effort over a collection of egotistical, narcissistic prima donnas who are more concerned with their own individual greatness. Like Walt Disney, Ed Catmull and John Lasseter understand that the quality of their work is not only going to endure for a day, a month, or a year, but rather for eternity. And that doesn't happen alone. Ed, John, and their Pixarian team are clearly making a dent in the universe!

"We have a company culture that celebrates being pioneers."

—John Lasseter

Bill and Lynn's Chalkboard

Complacent teams equal
mediocre results. Fully engaged
and "interested" teams equal
blockbuster results!

13

Ready, Set, Go!

GO TO ALMOST any playground and you may hear children's voices shouting, "Ready, set, go" to begin the race to the swing set, start the climb to the top of the jungle gym, or signal the start of a game of tag. If we could bottle the energy release when those words are spoken, we might free ourselves from a long-term dependence on fossil fuel!

By this stage in any given business book, the author has typically revealed the "10 Hard-Core Tools to Achieve . . ." or "7 Habits of Successful . . ." or "5 Disciplines for Customer . . ." or "3 Rules of . . ." Our initial thoughts for this chapter were to present something like, "10 Steps to Transform Any Company into an Innovation Giant." But the premise of this book is "lessons from the corporate playground" and how we can reawaken and apply the childlike innovative spirit that lives deep within us.

Children who go out for recess in the morning don't gather their classmates together and say, "Let's get our aerobic workout this morning playing tag and this afternoon work on upper body muscle development on the monkey bars." What happens is that they hit the playground and someone says, "Let's play tag or kick ball" or whatever game that comes to mind. It just happens. No one follows a 10-, 7-, 5-, or 3-point plan for innovation. The important thing is that the school has created an environment that encourages innovation—allows free time to play, provides the equipment, and of course, provides the classmates. If recess were eliminated or replaced with a highly structured activity, for example, tag is played on Monday, Wednesday, and Friday; and kick ball is played on Tuesday and Thursday, that innovative spirit—like in many corporate environments—would soon evaporate.

A number of organizations apply a highly structured process to their innovation projects. Pixar, Disney, and Whirlpool have employed standardized project plans that have various structures, required documentation, and milestones. (The Disney Nine-Step Process and the Whirlpool Four-Step Process are outlined in our book *The Disney Way*). Projects in these companies often take from one to four years to complete and need somewhat of a structured approach. However, it is essential that the process be flexible enough to allow for truly innovative ideas. In 2001, if the Apple innovators had been told to simply redesign the portable CD player, the iPod would have never been developed. In those days, digital music players were too large to be practical and had an ineffective computer interface. Apple released their first portable iPod on October 23, 2001, and reinvented the entire music industry.

The point is that even with tight deadlines (the first iPod was developed by Apple in less than ten months) and a standardized innovation process, you must adopt a culture of mutual respect and trust in which people have the freedom to engage in open, creative dialogue.

Here are our keys to creating your own corporate playground. Remember: Innovate, don't imitate. . . . This is just a starting point!

1. The story is king. Ask any Pixar employee what their secret to success is, and they will tell you, "The story is king." Pixar's Craig Good said, "Story is king, and we mean it. The story gets worked out endlessly as simple storyboard drawings, then modelers build the sets, props, and characters on the computer." It does not matter if you are making movies, manufacturing refrigerators, or selling hot dogs; everyone, from the boardroom to the storeroom, should be first and foremost a three-dimensional Technicolor storyteller. First develop your story, then innovate around it.

2. Displayed thinking techniques—storyboarding. Generate ideas graphically, instead of just verbally, to expand team members' perspectives, sharpen their focus, and spur them to see, feel, and dream, not just think. The late award-winning Pixar director Joe Ranft once commented on storyboarding: "We [Pixar] are in the Disney tradition of storyboarding. In the early days, they developed their stories pretty much 100 percent through drawings [storyboards]. There's something that happens when you see it in a drawing that suggests new possibilities. There's something concrete. When you read it on a page, everyone's imagination is open to many possibilities. Or ten people can be in a meeting, read a script, and agree on it. The second you do a drawing of it, all the unseen potential problems, and all the unseen potential wealth in the scene can come out." Former Whirlpool project manager Jerry McColgin commented on using storyboarding to identify potential barriers to a successful and innovative project: "They [team members] don't want to stand up and talk about their doubts, so storyboarding is a way for people to get their thoughts on cards anonymously. It is a tremendously helpful technique for seeing a way to eliminate barriers." Learn and use storyboarding.

3. Improv (improvisation). Wikipedia defines *improvisation* as "the practice of acting and reacting, of making and creating, in the moment and in response to the stimulus of one's immediate environment. This can result in the invention of new thought patterns, new practices, new structures or symbols, and/or new ways to act." It should be of no surprise that Pixar University teaches improv. Randy Nelson said, "If you don't create an atmosphere in which risk can be easily taken, in which weird ideas can be floated, then it's likely you're going to be producing work that will look derivative in the marketplace. Those kind of irrational what-ifs eventually lead to something that makes you go, 'Wow, I never would have thought about it.'" Encourage, inspire, instigate, and teach improv.

4. Plus-ing. Walt Disney originally coined the term *plus-ing* as a way of making a film, attraction, or idea better. He told his cast members to keep looking for ways to improve even when they thought their work was really good. One of our favorite examples of Walt's plus-ing happened late one year at Disneyland. Walt had decided to hold a Christmas parade at his new park. Knowing that the parade would cost several hundred thousand dollars, Walt's brother Roy and the accountants tried to convince him not to spend the money on such an extravagant event. Their rationale was that park guests were already coming for the Christmas holiday, and no one expected a parade. Walt answered, "That's just the point—we should do the parade precisely *because* no one's expecting it. Our goal at Disneyland is to always give the people *more* than they expect. As long as we keep surprising them, they'll keep coming back. But if they ever stop coming, it'll cost us ten times that much to get them to come back." Like Walt Disney, Pixar makes plus-ing a way of life. Randy Nelson explains, "At Pixar what we mean by plus-ing is this: You take a piece of work, something you are working on collaboratively, and when they give it to you, you don't judge it. You say, 'How do I plus this, how do I accept the offer and make my partner look good?'" Always look for ways to plus your product or service. Never, ever accept "good enough."

5. Collaboration (inside). Randy Nelson stated, "Collaboration for Pixar means amplification—by hooking up a number of human beings who are listening to each other, are interested in each other, bring a separate depth to the problem, bring breadth that brings them interest in the entire solution, allows them to communicate on multiple different levels, verbally, in writing, in feeling, in acting, in pictures. And in all those ways, finding the most articulate way to get a high-fidelity notion across to a broad range of people so they can each pull on the right lever." Wow! What a definition. We just love those words, "high-fidelity notion across to a broad range of people." If your innovation team does not mirror your market, something is wrong. Too many new product innovation teams are made up of about twenty fiftyish white male engineers, one African American accountant, and one female marketing specialist. Don't diversify just because it is socially correct; do it because it makes good business sense. Women purchase 83 percent of all consumer products, determine 92 percent of vacation destinations, and make 80 percent of the health-care decisions. If women have this much buying power, doesn't it stand to reason that we form teams with a greater representation of women? Don't just collaborate—diversify!

6. Collaboration (outside). Find the wacky, "I'll try anything" customer to help develop that new, innovative high-fidelity notion. Find an equally wacky supplier to join in your quest for the high-fidelity notion.

7. Prototype. Try. Learn. Try again. A Fortune 100 CEO (who will remain nameless to protect him from the embarrassment) once spent $50 billion buying small companies throughout the nation that offered a product that he thought would complement his existing product line. Once the two product lines were bundled, a marketing study revealed that his customers would not buy the two product lines as a bundled package. The $50 billion "experiment" was sold at a considerable loss. We asked this CEO why he didn't try bundling these two products in a small marketplace to test the customers' reactions. He could have performed one heck of a prototype for a mere $1 billion! His eyes glazed over. The problem was that some of the company executives thought they knew more than their customers. Wrong! He who fails most, wins. This CEO only failed once, and he lost. Pixar director Pete Docter commented, "All our films are failures at some point in the process." Prototype . . . Try . . . Learn . . . Try again. Prototype . . . Try . . . Learn . . . Try again. Prototype . . . Try . . . Get the picture?

8. Working on cool projects. There is no such thing as a boring project, only boring project teams. Assume your company is going to remodel your place of business. Your team is assigned the task of redesigning the parking lot. The team could look at this task in two different ways.

First they may say, "Boring. Why couldn't we work on a more exciting area like the company atrium?" With this attitude, they would more than likely end up designing a boring, run-of-the-mill parking facility like any other you have seen. Or they could say, "Wow, this is really cool. This is the first impression our customers have of our company." With this "cool" attitude, the team would more than likely come up with an innovative design that could incorporate soothing music, exotic landscaping, fun signage, flashy colors, outdoor video screens. Boring Teams = Boring Products. Cool Teams = Cool Products. Make every innovative project an exhilarating, inspiring, and compelling experience.

9. **Training.** Pixar believes that every worker has unlimited potential. To help unleash this potential, they offer more than a hundred classes at Pixar University. As we stated earlier, employees are encouraged to attend four hours of ongoing education each week on company time. Design your own learning environment that engages the full commitment and creativity of all employees.

10. **Fun. Play.** The level of fun and play we have in the workplace is a function of our attitude. *Attitude* can be defined as our demeanor, mind-set, mood, stance, or temperament. We choose our mind-set—are we going to be happy, have fun, and make work play, or are we going to be angry, woeful, and make work a drudgery? Life is too short not to enjoy what you do. Have fun. Play!

11. **Transparency (show and tell).** Transparency in business innovation refers to removing all barriers to

information, rules, data, and people. It also means that nearly all decision making is carried out publicly. Pixar president Ed Catmull explains, "[In] our daily review process, people show work in an incomplete state to the whole animation crew, and although the director makes decisions, everyone is encouraged to comment." Decisions are not made behind the scenes by the suits (or in John Lasseter's case, the Hawaiian shirt). If you have to refer to the organizational chart to get permission to talk to someone, you do not have transparency. As Ed stated, "Decision-making hierarchy and communication structure in organizations are two different things." Remove the barriers to information and communication in your organization.

12. Celebrations. Big dreams call for big celebrations. Take every chance to celebrate birthdays, milestone achievements, even failures. Phil Daniels, a successful Sydney, Australia, businessman, said, "Reward excellent failures. Punish mediocre successes." Celebrations help create and promote an environment conducive to innovation.

13. Brain trust. Ed Catmull commented on Pixar's brain trust: "When a director and producer feel in need of assistance, they convene the group [eight directors and anyone else they think would be valuable] and show the current version of the work in progress followed by a lively two-hour give-and-take discussion, which is all about making the movie better. . . . After a session, it's up to the director of the movie and his or her team to

decide what to do with the advice; there are no manda-
tory notes, and the brain trust has no authority." If your
company does not or will not form a formal brain trust,
form your own. Your brain trust should be a group of
fellow "radical," free-thinking activists who are willing
to dream big.

14. Dreamers with deadlines. Author and management expert Warren Bennis calls innovators "dreamers
with deadlines." Despite our remarks about standard
innovation process plans being too rigid, it is important
to adhere to timelines and milestones. That should not
be an excuse for small dreams, a mediocre product, or
an unhappy team. Like professional sports, innovation
is serious business, but the great sports teams dream
big, work to uncompromising deadlines, find innovative
ways to win, and have fun accomplishing their dreams.
Your innovation team should do the same.

15. Postmortems. At the end of each project, identify
five things you would do differently and five things you
would repeat. Pixar uses this postmortem technique
at the completion of each of its films. Ed Catmull said,
"The balance between the positive and the negative helps
make it a safer environment. . . . [We] employ lots of data
in the review. Because we're a creative organization,
people tend to assume that much of what we do can't be
measured or analyzed. That's wrong. . . . We keep track
of the rates at which things happen, how often something has to be reworked, whether a piece of work was

completely finished or not when it was sent to another department, and so on. Data can show things in a neutral way, which can stimulate discussion and challenge assumptions arising from personal impressions. . . . Our job is to solve problems even when we're successful. If you don't, you will fail." Learn from all experiences.
16. Quality is the best business plan. What more can we say? Once you compromise quality, you are dead in the water.

If you embrace these sixteen fundamentals, you will be well on your way to creating a culture of innovation. For our nation or any nation to compete in this new century or for infinity and beyond, we must move from the current age of risk-aversive short-term business mentality to an age of really cool new product and service experiences.

Step back and consider our country's economic development. We began as an agrarian society with 90 percent of the population employed in farming. Today, less than 2 percent are employed in farming, and yet we export almost $60 billion annually in crops. The agrarian society was replaced by the industrial era. Manufacturing employment reached its peak in the 1920s. By 1950, we were in the service era, followed in 1970 by the information age (risk-aversive, short-term business mentality being a subset of this). We are now entering into an age of rapid innovation.

To be competitive in this new age, the United States must rekindle the spirit of entrepreneurialism that once made us great. Our old Yankee "Know How!" has turned into Yankee "No, How?" We are at serious risk of losing our passion for developing innovative products and service experiences . . . and believe it or not, the new "patent mentality" is a key culprit! From 2007 to 2008, the number of patents granted of U.S. origin was down 1.8 percent, those of foreign origin up 4.5 percent. In 2008, the number of foreign patents exceeded the number of U.S. patents by 9 percent. (This was the first time in the history of the patent office that the number of foreign patents exceeded the number of U.S. patents.)

If these statistics are not bad enough, consider this. Many of our past innovative organizations have gone from research *and* development to *just* research. They have become "patent factories" where the output is not a "knock your socks off" over-the-top product or service—it is simply the patent. Instead of jumping in the water to develop the product, organizations are obsessed with selling patents, too afraid to take the risk and bring exciting products to market. IBM earns more than $1 billion a year from its patents; HP earns more than $200 million from selling patents. In 1990, Microsoft had only three patents. On January 20, 2009, Microsoft celebrated its 10,000th patent. They have an entire corporate division dedicated to selling patents and investigating patent infringement. Instead of employing the Walt Disneys, Henry Fords, Ed Catmulls, Alvy Ray Smiths, and John Lasseters, these companies are employing Harvard-trained patent lawyers and certified public accountants to sell and manage patents. Rather than developing the next series of "wow" factor products and experiences, these companies fail to rekindle their entrepreneurial innovative spirit.

Open-minded, imaginative consumers are now clamoring for exciting new products. The leaders of tomorrow will be the ones who don't sell out for quick and easy profits from risk-averse products, but rather will create the next wave of cool products such as the GPS, Wii, iPhone, or Kindle e-reader.

If we all are to be creative leaders, we must continually be on the cutting edge, and Pixar and Disney are shining examples of doing just that! In 2008, they announced a substantial research and development collaboration with Carnegie Mellon University and the Swiss Federal Institute of Technology. World-class science and technology academic talent will partner with virtually all the key business units—studios, media networks, theme parks, and resorts—of this multinational company. Ed Catmull made the announcement at the annual SIGGRAPH computer graphics conference: "Creating the next generation of sophisticated technologies requires long-term vision and collaboration with world-class innovators."

"Thinking is easy, acting is difficult, and to put one's

thoughts into action is the most difficult thing in the

world. Knowing is not enough; we must apply. Willing

is not enough; we must do."

—Johann Wolfgang von Goethe, German philosopher

Our dream is that—as our friends at Pixar and OMA have done—you will open your mind to creating innovative and exciting ways to enrich the lives of both your customers and your entire organization. Ed Catmull says that he is not in the film business just to make money or win awards. His passion for his work is evident in his heartfelt statement, "I really want to make movies that touch people and make them better. Otherwise, what are we doing here?"

We hope that *Innovate the Pixar Way* inspires you to create your own innovative playground that will, as Ed said, "touch people and make them better." Make your childlike **dreams** come true, **believe** in yourself and your playmates, **dare** to jump in the water, and **do** start making a real difference!

Ready, set, go! Begin unleashing your

enormous childlike energy on the world!

Bill and Lynn's Chalkboard

Innovation cannot be ordered
like a pizza. It requires
dedicated leadership and
a collaborative culture!

Other Corporate Playgrounds

DON'T CLOSE THIS book thinking that only Pixar has the corner on the "fun" market! Here are six diverse and tremendously successful organizations that are not only serious about innovation but also energize and inspire their team members to embrace a childlike spirit of fun.

Google

Niche: Google began in January 1996 as a research project by Larry Page and Sergey Brin, fellow Stanford Ph.D. students and close friends. Together they hypothesized that a search engine that analyzed the relationships between websites would produce better results than existing techniques (existing search engines at the time essentially ranked results according to how many times the search term appeared on a page). Today, Google Inc. is an American public corporation that earns revenue from advertising related to its Internet search, e-mail, online mapping, office productivity, social-networking and video-sharing services as well as selling advertising-free versions of the same technologies. Based in Mountain View, California, the company, whose headquarters is known as the Googleplex, has approximately twenty thousand full-time employees.

Culture at a Glance
* Mission: "To organize the world's information and make it universally accessible and useful."
* Core values:
  * We want to work with great people.
  * Technology innovation is our lifeblood.
  * Working at Google is fun.
  * Be actively involved; you are Google.
  * Don't take success for granted.
  * Do the right thing; don't be evil.

- ◆ Earn customer and user loyalty and respect every day.
- ◆ Sustainable long-term growth and profitability are key to our success.
- ◆ Google cares about and supports the communities where we work and live.
- ◆ We aspire to improve and change the world.
- ◆ Top ten reasons to work at Google:
  - ◆ Lend a helping hand.
  - ◆ Life is beautiful.
  - ◆ Appreciation is the best motivation.
  - ◆ Work and play are not mutually exclusive.
  - ◆ We love our employees, and we want them to know it.
  - ◆ Innovation is our bloodline.
  - ◆ Good company everywhere you look.
  - ◆ Uniting the world, one user at a time.
  - ◆ Boldly go where no one has gone before.
  - ◆ There is such a thing as a free lunch after all.
- ◆ Recruit people who show signs of "Googleyness"— are able to work effectively in a flat organization and in small teams; respond to a fast-paced changing environment; are well-rounded and possessing unique interests and talents to innovate; possess enthusiasm for the challenge of making the world a better place.
- ◆ All engineers may devote 20 percent of their time, approximately one day every week, to any project they choose.

- A $500 take-out food benefit can be used within the first four weeks of an employee's leave of absence with a new baby.
- Free gourmet meals—breakfast, lunch, and dinner—every day!
- Quarterly department off-site experiences are planned for teams to bond together and have fun.
- Google offices resemble those at Pixar—Lava lamps, couches, funny signage, and so on.

Fun Facts

- The name Google is a play on the word *googol*, coined by Milton Sirotta, nephew of American mathematician Edward Kasner. A googol refers to the number represented by 1 followed by a 100 zeros. It's a very large number. In fact, there isn't a googol of anything in the universe—not stars, not dust particles, not atoms. The verb "google" was added to *Merriam-Webster's Collegiate Dictionary* and the *Oxford English Dictionary* in 2006, meaning "to use the Google search engine to obtain information on the Internet." Google's use of the term reflects its mission to organize the world's immense (seemingly infinite) amount of information and make it universally accessible and useful.
- Google's search engine was originally nicknamed "BackRub" because the system checked "backlinks" to estimate the importance of a site.

- In 1999, Google hired Charlie Ayers as the first chef. He won the job in a cook-off judged by the company's forty employees. His previous claim to fame was catering for the legendary rock group the Grateful Dead. Charlie was the fifty-sixth employee at Google when he arrived in 1999. By the time he left the company in May 2005, he oversaw a kitchen staff of 135, serving four thousand meals a day and organizing parties and events for the growing Google workforce.

Cool Quotes

- Larry Page, cofounder: "We think a lot about how to maintain our culture and the fun elements. I don't know if other companies care as much about those things as we do."
- Claire Stapleton, pubic affairs associate: "People are more productive when they're working on projects that really excite them. . . . When you give people the chance to apply their passion to the company, they can do amazing things. It's the same idea with our perks—organic cafés, lecture series, yoga classes— great things are more likely to happen in the right culture and environment."
- An employee: "Google is a great company and I am very proud to be a part of it. The perks are extraordinary and this is the most unique working environment I have ever been in. The products, ideas,

creative minds that we have continue to amaze and inspire me."

♦ Eric Schmidt, CEO, when asked about the core value "Don't be evil": "When I joined the company [I thought] this was crap; companies don't have these things. I thought it was a joke. It must be a Larry and Sergey thing. So I was sitting in a room six months in, and an engineer said, 'That's evil.' It's like a bomb goes off in the room. Everybody has a moral and ethical discussion that, by the way, stopped the product."

Griffin Hospital

Niche: Griffin Hospital is a 160-bed acute-care, not-for-profit community hospital located in Derby, Connecticut. In June 1994 the hospital opened the first patient care building in the country designed and constructed to accommodate a Planetree care philosophy. Planetree is an international, nonprofit consumer health organization whose vision is to humanize and demystify the health-care experience and is a subsidiary of Griffin Health Services Corporation. Griffin's facility and care model have set a new standard for hospitals and architects. Griffin has won the 1995 Design Award from The Center for Health Design, which recognizes design that promotes well-being and healing; the American Hospital Association, American Society for Healthcare Engineering 1996 VISTA Award for new construction; and the New England Hospital Assem-

bly 1996 top-design award sponsored by the Boston Society
of Architects. Groups from more than five hundred hospitals, both domestic and foreign, have visited Griffin since
1994.

Culture at a Glance

- Mission: "To provide personalized, humanistic,
  consumer-driven health care in a healing environ-
  ment; to empower individuals to be actively involved
  in decisions affecting their care and well-being
  through access to information and education; and to
  provide leadership to improve the health of the community we serve."
- Core values:
  - Quality and service
  - Respect and dignity
  - Collaboration
  - Entrepreneurship and innovation
  - Stewardship
- Practice patient empowerment, open medical
  records, and formal care conferences.
- For this year's celebration for being recognized as
  one of *Fortune*'s "100 Best Companies to Work For,"
  employees led an initiative to contribute funds—
  money that for the past nine years had been spent on
  them as a reward for this honor—to assist commu-
  nity residents in need.
- Special spontaneous celebrations are held for
  remarkable achievement. Division vice presi-

dents provide pizza parties or cakes to department employees.

♦ A celebration is held for each department selected as Department of the Quarter. Winning departments (four per year) make presentations to the executive staff in support of their selection as Department of the Year. The competition is intense and the presentations are very creative and a lot of fun for both the department presenters and the executive staff.

♦ Planetree Cart—Griffin's engineering department built a Planetree Cart that can be taken to a specific department or through the entire hospital to say "thank you" on particularly high-volume or high-stress days. The Planetree Cart can carry beverages, ice cream, sandwiches, or other special goodies.

♦ Annual Planetree Day for staff and visitors—Planetree Day was established as a way of introducing the public and Griffin employees to the Planetree philosophy of care and to showcase complementary and holistic health programs including guided imaging, therapeutic touch, acupuncture and Eastern medicine, aromatherapy, and so forth. Free blood pressure and cholesterol checks are offered. Griffin staff members serve as hosts and presenters.

Fun Facts

♦ Griffin is the only hospital in the country ever to be named to *Fortune*'s "100 Best Companies to Work For" list for ten consecutive years.

- In the 1980s, Griffin was trying to reinvent their maternity ward patient experience. CEO Patrick Charmel and a Griffin marketing manager turned themselves into "secret shoppers" to benchmark other hospitals. Posing as husband and pregnant wife, they contacted several hospitals around the country and pretended to be shopping for an obstetrician and a hospital suitable for delivering their child.
- Griffin uses the overhead sound system to play the Brahms lullaby for each new birth in the Childbirth Center. The entire Griffin family looks forward to the "birth announcements."

Cool Quotes

- Bill Powanda, vice president: Griffin Hospital's employees use good judgment and creativity in their interactions with patients, all without a script. As Bill explains, "When other hospitals visit Griffin, they give us high praise for the lack of 'scripting' in our environment, saying Griffin seemed more sincere than other hospitals that employ scripting for their specific departments. What our guests are seeing is evidence that Griffin's genuine customer service approach was always part of its culture."
- Patrick Charmel, CEO: "Today when patients come here, they expect a superior patient experience. Certainly they expect to have a good surgical outcome, but they also want a good experience. They want a

friendly environment that smells good; they want great food, their families embraced, their questions answered."

Men's Wearhouse

Niche: Men's Wearhouse is one of the largest specialty retailers of men's business and formal attire and operates more than 1,200 stores throughout North America and some 490 stores that sell and rent tuxedos nationwide. Men's Wearhouse sells tailored suits typically priced 10 percent to 20 percent less than department stores, as well as shoes, formal wear, and casual clothes. Its K&G subsidiary caters to thriftier shoppers and sells women's career apparel in most of its 100-plus stores.

Culture at a Glance
+ Mission: "To maximize sales, provide value to our customers, and deliver top-quality customer service, while still having fun and maintaining our values."
+ Critical values:
    + Nurturing creativity
    + Growing together
    + Admitting to our mistakes
    + Promoting a happy and healthy lifestyle
    + Enhancing a sense of community
    + Striving toward becoming self-actualized people

- The Corporate Philosophy statement promotes their culture of "Servant Leadership": "When mistakes are made, leaders focus first on their coaching role, not their umpire role. Mistakes are opportunities for both mentoring and learning—not for instilling fear into the workplace. Reducing fear draws out our employees' best efforts and most positive attitudes."
- Founder George Zimmer's famous trademark line "You're going to like the way you look. I guarantee it." (Part of the Men's Wearhouse Value Commitment is great wardrobe consulting. George is an authentic guy who totally believes what he says!)
- Promotes celebrations

Fun Facts
- After George Zimmer graduated from college, he joined his dad's apparel-manufacturing company based in Dallas, Texas. George opened the first Men's Wearhouse store with his college roommates in Houston, Texas. The merchandise consisted largely of polyester sport coats from his father's company. Since he was unable to afford a cash register, he used a cigar box on his first day of business.
- George's fellow classmate was Harold Ramis who cowrote the hilariously funny 1978 movie classic *Animal House* that starred the late John Belushi, one of the brightest stars of NBC's "Saturday Night Live."
- Pixar rents and purchases Men's Wearhouse tuxedos for their black tie film release celebrations!

Cool Quotes

- George Zimmer, founder and CEO: "It all comes down to being able to get spirit and enthusiasm from people. It's impossible to measure, so it's been overlooked in business. Enjoying life and celebrating lead to being enthusiastic about what you are doing forty hours a week."

- Julie Panaccione, vice president of corporate culture: "The spirit of the company is nurtured by building a values-based corporate culture where employees are the number one stakeholder. I think we recognize that because people do spend a lot of time at work in the store environment, if it's not fun, it can become monotonous. If you are going to spend that much time with people, you need to build these relationships . . . and having fun at work is such a big part of that. It's not uncommon in a Men's Wearhouse . . . to have a Ping-Pong table set on top of the tie laydown table. So, in a store they might have an area where a gentleman buys a suit, they put shirts on top, they put ties on top, belts on top, but when there's no customers in the store or even if there are customers in the store, it turns into a Ping-Pong table. We do have a kind of playground at our workplace."

- Doug Ewert, president and chief operating officer: "When the company was busting at the seams with growth in early 2000 . . . George sent out an edict saying 'the pool table stays.'"

- Julie Panaccione: "Each one of our stores gets a social spirit budget that encourages camaraderie and fun out in the field. We can't go out into the field every week because we have over a thousand locations, so we have events regionalized. On June 7 . . . we are having a . . . Strike Night. It's a bowling event for every store employee, so they can go out and bowl in their local AMF center."
- Julie Panaccione: "The company prides itself on having a very open door communications policy. The top people encourage people to get to them . . . [to communicate] a sales idea, a contest idea, an idea about a party or an event. This year, we gave a $10,000 award for an innovative idea. We put a contest out in the field and said, 'If you have an innovative idea to save the company money . . . please let us know.' We got thousands of applications from Canada and the United States. Our employees have a great deal of trust for the management of the company, and the management of the company has a great deal of trust in the employees. . . . It's a great value system."

Nike

Niche: Nike is the world's number one shoemaker. It designs and sells shoes for a variety of sports, including baseball, cheerleading, golf, volleyball, hiking, tennis, and football.

Nike also sells Cole Haan dress and casual shoes, as well as athletic apparel and equipment. In addition, Nike operates Niketown shoe and sportswear stores, Nike factory outlets, and Nike Women shops. Nike sells its products throughout the United States and in more than 180 other countries. In 2007, Nike bought British soccer retailer Umbro.

Culture at a Glance

◆ Mission: "To bring inspiration and innovation to every athlete in the world. If you have a body, you are an athlete."

◆ Playfully, deliberately, and cleverly—that's how Nike sustains a *fun* business culture that celebrates the "kid within."

   ◆ "Playfully" example: Once a month throughout the spring and summer, the company promotes Thirst Thursday. It's an unpredictable and highly entertaining playfest where an employee-led house band plays during such games as H-O-R-S-E between a Nike Hoops Star and a summer intern.

   ◆ "Deliberately" and "Cleverly" example: Nike runs its business and all of its sports industry endeavors by following eleven simple truths, called Maxims:

      1. It is our nature to innovate.
      2. Nike is a company.
      3. Nike is a brand.
      4. Simplify and go.

5. The consumer decides.
6. Be a sponge.
7. Evolve immediately.
8. Do the right thing.
9. Master the fundamentals.
10. We are on the offense. Always.
11. Remember the man.

• "Playfully, Deliberately, and Cleverly" example: The Maxim Awards are a recognition program akin to the Academy Awards celebration. Employees vote on Nike business innovations based on the eleven Maxims. The Maxim Awards are a raucous, irreverent night of celebration and recognition.

Examples were provided by Kevin Carroll, former Nike "Katalyst," the man hired to nurture and care for the company's inner spirit, to provoke new ways of thinking, and to motivate and inspire—wow, what a job! Kevin is also the author of *Rules of the Red Rubber Ball* and *The Red Rubber Ball at Work*.

Fun Facts

• Nike is the name of the Greek goddess of victory. The name came to Jeff Johnson, the company's first employee, in his sleep.
• The Swoosh logo was designed for a fee of $35 by a young design student in Portland, Oregon. Later, she was given some Nike stock.

◆ The "Just Do It" line was conceived by advertising copywriter Dan Wieden.

Cool Quotes

◆ Mark Parker, president and CEO: "As we look at how we design and develop products and run our global business, it's not enough to be solving the challenges of today. We are designing for the sustainable economy of tomorrow, and for us that means using fewer resources, more sustainable materials, and renewable energy to produce new products."

◆ Scott Bedbury, former marketing chief and the man who launched Nike's "Just Do It" slogan: "In some companies, there is a line item called 'Brand' and a bigger line item called 'Product.' At Nike, there [is] no separation. You need to be a storyteller of your brand . . . but with one brand voice."

◆ Kevin Carroll: "Nike's ability to purposely inject playful and inspirational moments for their global team members allows the Nike brand to consistently be an industry leader in product design and creative brand messaging."

Target

Niche: Target Corporation is an American retailing company that was founded in Minneapolis, Minnesota, in 1902 as Goodfellow Dry Goods. In 1962, the first Target store opened in Roseville, Minnesota, and in 2000 the parent company changed its name from Dayton Hudson to Target. Today, Target operates approximately 1,700 stores in forty-nine states nationwide, including more than 240 SuperTarget stores.

Culture at Glance

♦ Mission: "To make Target the preferred shopping destination for our guests by delivering outstanding value, continuous innovation, and an exceptional guest experience by consistently fulfilling our 'Expect More. Pay Less.' brand promise. To support our mission, we are guided by our commitments to great value, the community, diversity, and the environment."

♦ Core values:

  ♦ Be fast, fun, and friendly.

  ♦ Foster an inclusive culture.

  ♦ Pursue leadership excellence.

  ♦ Embrace speed is life.

  ♦ Advance our reputation.

♦ "Targeteers"—the trend-merchandising team that tracks trends around the globe and tries to anticipate changing consumer tastes. (They benchmarked The Walt Disney Company and the Disney Imagineers!)

♦ Have developed roughly ten to twelve Target brands in apparel and accessories

eye, was inspired by John Lasseter's Hawaiian shirt
collection.
  - Bullseye prefers the climate of Los Angeles over
Minneapolis (corporate headquarters) and has been
afforded first-class travel on many airlines.

Cool Quotes

  - Michael Alexin, vice president of product design and
development: "Innovation is one of our core values.
It sounds trite, everyone says this, but we really live
it. The way we work at Target is a lot of the ideas
bubble from the bottom up. It's not a top-down organization. At the top, we think clear vision and strategy, but we try to create a culture of idea acceptance,
not idea judgment. Knowing that we have very clear
parameters for financial success, we do a tremendous amount of ideation and testing to see what will
really excite and capture the attention of our guests,
our customers, or entertain them in a different way
or sometimes to provide solutions to problems they
don't even know they have."
  - Michael Alexin: "Our motto at Target is FFF—fast,
fun, friendly. Every division has an FFF team with an
FFF captain, and we are wacky. For the United Way
campaign last year, we got a couple of hundred what
we call naked Target Bullseye dogs and we had a contest for the proceeds going to the United Way. These

people got together and designed an outfit, and now we have a whole collection of . . . these amazing bulldogs . . . like Pablo Picasso bulldogs."

◆ Jodee Koziak, executive vice president of human resources: "FFF is our brand personality. It's kind of a mojo that we have and drives a lot of positive behavior in terms of a respectful, innovative, and surprising culture . . . from being open to a difference of thought and making sure that you are driving more of an inclusive approach not only to diversity, ethnicity, and multiculturalism, but getting different points of view out on the table in really fun and appealing ways."

◆ Kari Thompson, director of corporate communications: "We take a very strategic approach to listening to our guests and acting on feedback. One of the ways we innovate that guest experience is with our store prototypes. We are always looking ahead to see what that experience, physically, needs to look and feel like. That's an ongoing process at Target."

◆ Michael Francis, chief marketing officer and executive vice president of marketing: "There is great participation and ownership of our strategy, and that has kept team members truly engaged and passionate for what they do. And that passion not only breeds innovation but commitment and a focus on the guest. . . . We continue to be able to win with the guest over time."

Zappos

Niche: In 1999, CEO Tony Hsieh helped start Zappos as an online shoe store, and the company subsequently expanded to offering a wide variety of goods. Zappos booked $1 billion in gross sales in 2008, 20 percent better than the year before. It has been profitable since 2006. Zappos, now the leading online shoe retailer, has 1,300 employees and is headquartered in Henderson, Nevada.

Culture at a Glance

- Unofficial mission: "Be amazing." (Tony doesn't really believe in formal mission statements!)
- Core values:
  - Deliver "wow" through service.
  - Embrace and drive change.
  - Create fun and a little weirdness.
  - Be adventurous, creative, and open-minded.
  - Pursue growth and learning.
  - Build open and honest relationships with communication.
  - Build a positive team and family spirit.
  - Do more with less.
  - Be passionate and determined.
  - Be humble.
- The company publishes an annual "Culture Book" in which employees describe what the culture means to them.

- Employee interviews have been held in places such as Lavo, a trendy Las Vegas nightclub, and over shots of vodka. Employees rate themselves on a scale of 1 to 10 on questions including, "How weird are you?" and "What was your last position called? Was that an appropriate title?" The company seeks out "weird" people (determined by the first question) and "uncomplaining, humble" people (determined by the second question).

- New corporate trainees experience four weeks of customer loyalty training that includes answering phones in the call center. This happens before starting their real jobs. After the training, Zappos offers them $2,000 to leave the company—no questions asked. This practice is to ensure that the new hires are more passionate about Zappos than they are the money. Nearly 97 percent of the trainees decline what Zappos calls "the Offer."

- The company promotes internal "parades" that feature random acts of kindness for randomly targeted employees, complete with bullhorn callouts, a funky hat, and a gift card.

- Spirit Week is kicked off by Mismatch Day where employees wear socks, clothes, and shoes that don't match.

Fun Facts

◆ Zappos CEO Tony Hsieh met his COO/CFO Alfred
   Lin in college, when Tony was running a pizza business and Alfred was his number one customer.

◆ The name Zappos is a play on *zapatos*, the Spanish
   word for "shoes."

◆ Zappos bathrooms are decorated with "urine color"
   charts, encouraging wackiness and fun.

◆ For the first five years of the company, the accounting department ran its books off the program easily
   found at many local stores: QuickBooks. Yes, Zappos
   was running a seventy million dollar business on a
   program most people use for personal or very small
   business operations.

◆ In 2009 Zappos debuted at No. 23 on *Fortune's* list
   of "100 Best Companies to Work For"—the highest-
   ranking newcomer!

Cool Quotes

◆ Tony Hsieh, CEO: "We've found that a fun atmosphere makes for happier employees, and happier
   employees are more productive and engaged than
   unhappy employees. Because of our fun, family-like
   culture, the level of trust is higher, communication
   is better, and overall employees are more productive
   and work harder."

◆ Alfred Lin, COO/CFO: "I often joke with Tony, 'We
   don't have any really original ideas.' What we really
   do well—we try to learn as much as we can from

everybody we meet and every company we see. That's what has allowed us to stay sort of nimble."

◆ Tony Hsieh: "Our number one focus is our company culture. We interview people for culture fit. We want people who are passionate about what Zappos is about—service. I don't care if they're passionate about shoes."

APPENDIX B

Bill and Lynn's Favorite Fun Facts About Pixar

♦ *Luxo Jr.* was Pixar's first film and made its debut at the 1986 SIGGRAPH annual film show. It is a computer-animated short film that is two and a half minutes, including credits. The film inspired Pixar's corporate mascot and logo, a small hopping desk lamp that has "hosted" every Pixar movie from *Toy Story* on. Pixar moviegoers are accustomed to seeing this adorable little lamp hop onto the screen before the opening credits and turn out the light after the closing credits. Leonard Maltin, one of the country's most recognized film critics, equated the lamp character to Mickey Mouse.

♦ John Lasseter once drove to the Academy Awards ceremony in the Oscar Meyer Weiner Mobile.

- John keeps his Oscars at home and has custom-made seasonal outfits for each (including a tux for Oscar night).
- Animator Andrew Gordon once noticed a small door near the floor of his office that was a vent shaft, an air-conditioning access area. He had to crawl through the door like Alice in Wonderland to get in, but he discovered that it was quite large inside. Andrew asked for and was granted permission to use his exciting new "office" space. He cleaned out all the dust and strung Christmas lights, then brought in animal-print upholstery, cushioned seating, mood lighting, and a bar. It became known as the "Love Lounge." Word of the fun new "hot spot" spread throughout the company, and soon invitations became a coveted commodity. The space became a regular stop for visiting notables, whose signatures covered the walls. In describing his first visit, actor Tim Allen said, "So, here is John Lasseter, Steve Jobs, and myself, and Steve goes, 'Let's go to the Love Lounge.' We had to crawl on all fours, three grown men, butt-to-nose, through this little hole in the wall. And there are lava lamps and pictures of Doris Day and stuff."
- John Ratzenberger has lent his voice to every Pixar movie to date, from Hamm in *Toy Story* to Foreman Tom in *Up*.
- Pixar was actively pursuing Bill Murray for the role of *Toy Story*'s Buzz Lightyear, but Murray lost the

producer's phone numbers . . . and lost the role to
Tim Allen!

◆ In April 2008, *Toy Story* made its debut as a live-
action musical on Disney Cruise Line's *The Disney
Wonder*. The musical features seven songs, including six originals and Randy Newman's "You've Got a
Friend in Me."

◆ While making *A Bug's Life*, the animation team
watched footage from a "bug cam" in order to perfect
their perspectives and colors.

◆ *Monsters, Inc.* was based on director Pete Docter's
childhood fears about monsters in the closet.

◆ In *Monsters, Inc.*, exactly 2,320,413 hairs comprise the
fur on the bearlike purple and blue, hairy and horned
monster Sulley!

◆ In *Finding Nemo*, a Buzz Lightyear doll can be seen
in the dentist's waiting room.

◆ In making *The Incredibles*, the animators created a
special program that seemed to light the characters
from within so as to create a human but comic-book
look.

◆ In preparing actor Spencer Fox for his role of Dash
in *The Incredibles*, director Brad Bird forced Fox to
run around the studio so he could capture on tape an
authentic out-of-breath voice.

◆ Computers used in the creation of *Cars* (2006) were
1,000 times faster than those used in *Toy Story*, just
eleven years earlier.

- In *Cars*, the original number for Lightning McQueen was going to be 57 in honor of John Lasseter's birth year, but it was later changed to 95 to represent the year Pixar's first movie, *Toy Story*, was released.
- In *Ratatouille*, the head chef, Skinner, was named after B. F. Skinner, the behavioral psychologist who experimented on rats.
- The name of the movie *WALL-E* is an acronym, standing for Waste Allocation Load Lifter–Earth-Class.
- When the Disney Imagineers decided to create an attraction based on *Toy Story* at Disney's Hollywood Studios, they built an entire district called *Pixar Place*—based on the Pixar Animation Studios in Emeryville, California. They exactly matched the color of the brick and mortar (details, details, details!) from the original Pixar Studios building in the construction of *Toy Story Midway Mania*. When Pixar venture capitalist Steve Jobs saw how much it looked like home, his eyes welled with tears.
- The Mr. Potato Head figure at *Toy Story Midway Mania* represents significant advances in Audio-Animatronic technology. Mr. Potato Head is the first such figure whose mouth appears to form actual words when he's talking. It's also the first Audio-Animatronic figure that can remove a body part and then reattach it (his ear).
- Award-winning screenwriter/director Tom McCarthy (*The Station Agent*, 2003) went to Pixar to work on *Up* for three months. *The Station Agent* was

actually one of the models for the story of *Up*. Tom helped develop the character of Russell, the Wilderness Explorer.

♦ The wilderness setting for *Up* was inspired by the *tepuis* (a table-top mountain) in Venezuela and Brazil.

Perhaps the most inspiring of all is so much more than a "fun fact." It encapsulates everything that Pixar stands for. In the words of John Lasseter:

> Let me tell you a funny story. I took the family to see this film one weekend. I'll go to see almost any film that's good for the whole family. And so we're sitting there watching this film, which I won't name, and there are long stretches that are just not very entertaining. My little son—he was probably six at the time—was sitting next to me, and right in the middle of this dull section, he turns to me and says, 'Dad? How many letters are in my name?' I must have laughed for five minutes. I thought, "Oh, man, this movie has lost this little boy. His mind has been wandering, trying to figure out how many letters there are in his name." So I told my wife, Nancy, what he said, and she started laughing, and then the story went down the row through my whole family, our four other sons, and we're sitting there as a family giggling and laughing. And I thought to myself, "If ever a child anywhere in the world leans over to their daddy during one of my movies and asks, 'How many letters are in my name?' I'll quit."

APPENDIX C

Through a Child's Eyes

Dream

"Too many people grow up. That's the real trouble with the world. They forget. They don't remember what it's like to be twelve years old."

—Walt Disney

Dream . . . Like a Child

Art by Marcia

"*I am an artist because I think that creating things is fun. When I draw things, I just imagine something, then draw it.*"

—Daniel

"*Dreams are things that inspire you.*"

—Anthony

"*I daydream about what could happen. . . . Dreams can actually really help you because they can help you think of new ideas that you can do or invent and stuff like that. And then you could be like the first person to go to the moon or something like that.*"

—Sharmila

All art and quotes courtesy of OMA grade school students.

Believe

"I don't believe in talking down to children. I don't believe in talking down to any certain segment."

—Walt Disney

Believe . . . in Your Playmates

Art by Carol

"When I make art I feel open and like anything can happen. Art is a very magical thing."

—Carol

"Usually in our class, everyone pitches in ideas. It's not like one person writing the entire opera; that's how it works."

—Taylor

"I enjoy being an artist because I could express my feelings whether it be sad, happy, angry, anything really. That is why I want to be an artist."

—Christian

"It's not just two people creating the whole opera; it's the whole class. And it's fun to audition for it, it's fun to get ready, it's fun to do all of it."

—Anthony

All art and quotes courtesy of OMA grade school students.

Dare

> *"Childishness? I think it's the equivalent of never*
>
> *losing your sense of humor. I mean, there's a certain*
>
> *something that you retain. It's the equivalent of not*
>
> *getting so stuffy that you can't laugh at others."*
>
> —Walt Disney

Dare . . . to Jump in the Water and Make Waves

Art by Zarit

"I like to play the violin to challenge myself. Dance is also a fun way to get out all my energy. I love being an artist."

—Mary

"It makes me really happy to be around people that act and just have fun."

—Anthony

"I go to daycare and there's like these monkey bars. Someone dared me to jump to the third bar, and now I can jump to the third bar but it was scary before that person dared me."

—Sharmila

All art and quotes courtesy of OMA grade school students.

Dare to Make a Difference: A Story

Many dedicated teachers have made a difference in the lives of their students, but OMA teacher Richard Leek may have saved the life of one of his students, Matthew. Their story begins when Matthew was in fourth grade and began his work with fellow OMA classmates learning to play the violin. The school district provided violins for each child in the class. Students were given instructions on how to care for their instruments and began to learn the basics of playing the violin. They were even allowed to take the instruments home. During the second week of instruction, Matthew brought his violin back to school and sheepishly gave it to Richard Leek, his OMA music teacher and violin instructor. The instrument had been smashed to pieces. Matthew made up some story—his brother had destroyed it, the dog had sat on it, whatever—so Richard just took the instrument without saying too much. Richard knew that Matthew came from a very troubled home where the parents had been separated and both had suffered from crystal meth addiction.

After considering the situation, Richard began to suspect that one of Matthew's parents more than likely had destroyed the violin in a drug-induced rage. With his own funds, Richard decided to purchase a replacement for the damaged violin. He sought out Matthew, handed him the new instrument, and said, "Let's begin again." After reviewing the instructions about the care of the violin, Richard added while looking Matthew straight in the eye,

"I see great promise in you." With that reassurance, Matthew began to think more seriously about the instrument and practiced harder and harder. He spent hours learning the music Richard gave him, and he progressed very rapidly, exceeding his classmates.

Matthew made his solo debut at age fourteen, and since then he has soloed with the Tucson and Buffalo Philharmonic Orchestras, was principal violinist with Interlochen Center for the Arts World Youth Symphony Orchestra, participated in the National Symphony Orchestra Youth Program at the John F. Kennedy Center on full scholarship, and continues to win numerous awards for his music.

Matthew told us, "Being part of the OMA program has changed my life. . . . It provided me a path in life and gave me a dream. . . . I would have never been exposed to it [music] without the OMA program. I owe my life to this program."

The story continues for his mentor. Richard Leek lost his wife to cancer during the time that he was mentoring Matthew. But because of his special connection with Matthew, he began to feel the purpose for his own life returning. Because of Matthew's family problems, Richard was named guardian and proceeded to adopt Matthew. Two lives were saved as a result.

Matthew told us he wants to play professionally, but that eventually he also wants to return to the Tucson Unified School District to give back to the children that follow him. Like Richard and Matthew, we should all "dare to make a difference."

Do

"Children are always reaching."

—Walt Disney

Do . . . Unleash Your Childlike Potential

Art by Daiveon

"My art is more surrealistic because reality gets so boring. In a way, I can go anywhere I want. That is why I am an artist."

—Daiveon

"I am really into making things. It's fun to do things like music and dancing and writing. And learning the parts to the opera. . . . I like the part I got a lot. It's one of the main characters actually. It's the prince!"

—Anthony

"I believe I can do anything, even if it is really, really hard. I can do it. I can always try to do something new!"

—Ana

All art and quotes courtesy of OMA grade school students.

References

Ackerman, Diane. *Deep Play*. New York: Vintage Books, 1999.

Adler, Shawn. "Pulling Back the Curtain at Pixar's Studios, Where 'Story Is King.'" *MTV Movie News,* November 6, 2006.

Alexin, Michael, vice president of product design and development, Target Corporation. Interview by the author, May 2009.

Ashcraft, Joan, Opening Minds Through the Arts cofounder; director of fine and performing arts, Tucson Unified School District. Interview by the author, April 2009.

Ask Student. "List of Google Core Values." askstudent.com, July 13, 2008.

Baker, Bob. "Eliminate the Elliptical!" newsthinking.com, July 13, 2006.

Barnes, Brooks. "After Years of Planning, a Major Expansion for Pixar's Bay Area Headquarters." http://carpetbagger.blogs.nytimes.com, April 22, 2009.

———. "Disney Expert Uses Science to Draw Boy Viewers." nytimes.com, April 14, 2009.

———. "Pixar Art Leaves Profit Watchers Edgy." nytimes.com, April 6, 2009.

Barsh, Joanna, Marla M. Capozzi, and Jonathan Davidson. "Leadership and Innovation." mckinseyquarterly.com, January 2008.

Billington, Alex. "Interview: Pixar and Disney Creative Chief John Lasseter." firstshowing.net, November 21, 2008.

Block, Alex Ben. "John Lasseter Leads Disney to Next Great Phase." hollywoodreporter.com, October 22, 2008.

Brew, Simon. "Will Pixar Regret Making *Up*?" genofgeek.com, April 30, 2009.

Brown, Stuart. *Play: How It Shapes the Brain, Opens the Imagination, and Invigorates the Soul.* With Christopher Vaughan. New York: Penguin Group, 2009.

Bughin, Jacques, Michael Chui, and Brad Johnson. "The Next Step in Open Innovation." mckinseyquarterly.com, June 2008.

Bunk, Matthew. "Sale Unlikely to Change Pixar Culture." insidebayarea.com, January 21, 2006.

Bunn, Austin. "Welcome to Pixar Planet." wired.com, No. 12.06, June 2004.

Burkeman, Oliver. "How Pixar Conquered the Planet." guardian.co.uk, November 12, 2004.

Can Magazine. "Interview: Andrew Jimenez on Pixar's One-Man Band." canmag.com, November 7, 2007.

Capodagli, Bill, and Lynn Jackson. *The Disney Way: Harnessing the Management Secrets of Disney in Your Company.* New York: McGraw-Hill, 2007.

———. *The Disney Way Fieldbook: How to Implement Walt Disney's Vision of "Dream, Believe, Dare, Do" in Your Own Company.* New York: McGraw-Hill, 2001.

Carey, Jesse. "John Lasseter: Stories That Live Forever." cbn. com.

Carmichael, Evan. "Lesson #4: Take Care of Your Team (Google)." evancarmichael.com.

Carroll, Kevin, former "Katalyst" for Nike; founder of The Katalyst Consultancy. Interview by the author, April 1, May 13, May 20, 2009.

Cartoon Brew. "The Art of Pixar Short Films: Interview with Amid Amidi." cartoonbrew.com, March 3, 2009.

Catmull, Ed. "How Pixar Fosters Collective Creativity." *Harvard Business Review* reprint, (September 2008).

Cesare, Anthony, first grade student at Duffy Elementary School, Tucson Unified School District. Interview by the author, April 2009.

Chafkin, Max. "The Zappos Way of Managing." inc.com, May 2009.

Conley, Chris. "Innovation All the Time." businessweek.com, September 19, 2006.

Creative Reaction. "In-House Training Is Pixar's Secret Weapon." creative-reaction.org, May 17, 2007.

Deming, W. Edwards. *Out of Crises*. Cambridge, MA: MIT Press, 1982.

Desowitz, Bill. "Catmull Offers Tech Talk." awn.com, February 28, 2009.

Dey, Sharmila, first grade student at Craigen Elementary School, Tucson Unified School District. Interview by the author, April 2009.

Dunne, Susan. "West Hartford Native Now Head of Marketing For Pixar." courant.com, May 3, 2009.

Edwards, Dustin. "Co-founder of Pixar Shares Tip for Entrepreneurs." http://business.nmsu.edu, March 9, 2009.

Eller, Claudia. "Disney's Low-Key Superhero." articles.latimes.com, June 12, 2006.

Ewert, Douglas, president and chief operating officer, Men's Wearhouse. Interview by the author, August 2001.

Fagen, Elizabeth, superintendent, Tucson Unified School District. Personal communication, May 2009.

Feeney, Mark. "Up up and away?" boston.com, May 24, 2009.

Francis, Michael, chief marketing officer and executive vice
    president of marketing, Target Corporation. Interview
    by the author, May 2009.
Fritz, Ben. "Disney Animation Gets Pixar-ization." variety.com,
    February 24, 2007.
Gagné, Michel. Personal communication, April 2009.
Gergen, Christopher, and Gregg Vanourek. "Zappos Culture
    Sows Spirit." washingtontimes.com, July 16, 2008.
Glenn, Robert, Jr. "The Cult and Culture of Zappos." inman.
    com, April 30, 2009.
———. "Pixar Defies Gravity." latimesblogs.latimes.com, June
    30, 2008.
Goldstein, Patrick. "Pixar's Secret Ingredient? Quality." latimes.
    com, July 1, 2008.
Google. "Top 10 Reasons to Work at Google." google.com, 2009.
Great Place to Work. "Why Is Google So Great?" greatplace
    towork.com, 2009.
Hawn, Carleen. "Pixar's Brad Bird on Fostering Innovation."
    gigaom.com, April 17, 2008.
Hill, Jim. "Toon Tuesday: The Story Behind 'The Pixar Story.'"
    http://jimhillmedia.com, November 1, 2008.
Hindo, Brian. "At 3M, a Struggle Between Efficiency and Cre-
    ativity." businessweek.com, June 11, 2007.
Hormby, Tom. "The Pixar Story: Dick Shoup, Alex Schure,
    George Lucas, Steve Jobs, and Disney." lowendmac.com,
    January 22, 2007.
Horn, John. "Secrets of Pixar's Inner Circle." latimes.com,
    March 12, 2008.
"How Companies Approach Innovation: A McKinsey Global
    Survey." mckinseyquarterly.com, October 2007.
Hsieh, Tony, chief executive officer, Zappos. Personal commu-
    nication, April 2009.
Hughes, Taylor Louise, fifth grade student at Corbett Elemen-
    tary School, Tucson Unified School District. Interview
    by the author, April 2009.

Internet Movie Database. "Trivia for *Toy Story*." imdb.com/ title/tt0114709/trivia, 1995.

"Interview with Ed Catmull." *Innovate*, February 2, 2007.

"Interview with Pixar TD Kim White Conducted by Eric Oehrl." *Frame by Frame* (Winter 1998).

Iwerks, Leslie. "The Pixar Story." *WALL-E* DVD, 2008.

Johnson, David. "Inside Animation—The Disney Art School— Part One." animationartist.com, 2000.

Jones, H. Eugene, Opening Minds through the Arts cofounder; main benefactor. Tucson Unified School District. Interview by the author, April 2009.

Kenyon, Heather. "10 Questions with Edwin Catmull, Super Genius." awn.com, No. 4.12, March 2000.

Kirsner, Scott. "Inventing the Movies: Hollywood's Epic Battle Between Innovation and the Status Quo, from Thomas Edison to Steve Jobs." *CreateSpace* (May 15, 2008).

Korkis, Jim. "The Birth of Animation Training." awn.com, September 23, 2004.

Koziak, Jodee, executive vice president of human resources, Target Corporation. Interview by the author, May 2009.

Kumar, Priya. "An Alumnus's Animated Career." diamond backonline.com, April 20, 2009.

Kurtzman, Joel. "An Interview with Warren Bennis." *Strategy+Business* (Third Quarter, 1997).

Lee, Ellen. "The Dynamic Duo Behind Pixar's Big Success." sfgate.com, January 29, 2006.

Letter from Steve Jobs to Shareholders, Annual Report, June 1998.

Lockhart, Andrew. "5 Lessons in Creativity from Pixar." thinkinginteractive.com, September 25, 2008.

Lohr, Steve. "Could Pixar Make It Without Disney?" nytimes. com, February 24, 1997.

Lynch, Larry. "Sustaining Innovation." encyclopedia.com, June 1, 2001.

Malhotra, Heide B. "Creativity and Eccentricity Thrive at
    Pixar." theepochtimes.com, June 21, 2008.
Marsland, Louise. "Everything Matters in Branding, Says Scott
    Bedbury." bizcommunity.com, June 20, 2006.
McGuinness, Mark. "Motivating Creative People—The Joy of
    Work." wishfulthinking.co.uk, November 3, 2008.
Mendonca, Lenny T., and Robert Sutton. "Succeeding at Open-
    Source Innovation: An Interview with Mozilla's Mitch-
    ell Baker." mckinseyquarterly.com, January 2008.
Movie Tome. "John Lasseter Quotes and Trivia." movietome.
    com, 2009.
"Music and Dance Drive Academic Achievement." *Edutopia:
    George Lucas Education Foundation.* edutopia.org, 2009.
Nelson, Randy. "Learning and Working in a Collaborative
    Age: A New Model for the Workplace." Keynote speech.
    Apple Education Leadership Summit, Edutopia: George
    Lucas Education Foundation, April 11, 2008.
"Nike's Considered Design Products." nikebiz.com, 2009.
North Star Manifesto. "Creative Visions Foundation—The
    Genius of Pixar—Top 10 Principles." blog.northstar
    manifesto.com, March 15, 2009.
Norton-Smith, Dulcinea. "Interesting Disney Pixar Trivia."
    suite101.com, March 24, 2008.
Olsen, Sander. "NYIT Computer Graphics Lab Turns 30." geek.
    com, March 19, 2004.
Online blogger. "A Unique, Exciting Internship Opportunity."
    ledova.com, October 3, 2008.
"The Original Spline Doctor." Drs. Andrew Gordon and Adam
    Burke interview with Ed Catmull, *Spline Doctors,*
    November 4, 2007.
Over Matter. "Craig Good (Pixar) Interview." overmatter.com,
    January 2, 2005.
Paik, Karen. *To Infinity and Beyond!: The Story of Pixar Anima-
    tion Studios.* San Francisco: Chronicle Books, 2007.

Panaccione, Julie, vice president of corporate culture, Men's Wearhouse. Interview by the author, May 2009.

Pecho, Bruce. "20 secrets of Disney's Hollywood Studios." chicagotribune.com, April 26, 2009.

Pfeuffer, Roger, former superintendent, Tucson Unified School District. Interview by the author, April 2009.

Pharma's Cutting Edge. "Pixar's Catmull Has Some Good Advice for Pharma Execs." pharmaweblog.com, September 2, 2008.

"Pixar: A Human Story of Computer Animation." Panel discussion with Brad Bird, Ed Catmull, Alvy Ray Smith, Andrew Stanton, and Michael Rubin. Computer History Museum, Mountain View, CA, May 16, 2005.

Poll, Donn, executive director of the Opening Minds through the Arts Foundation, Tucson Unified School District. Interview by the author, April 2009.

Powanda, William, vice president, Griffin Health Services, Griffin Hospital. Interview by the author, April 22, 2009.

Price, David A. *The Pixar Touch: The Making of a Company.* New York: Alfred A. Knopf, 2008.

Prokesch, Steve. "Building a 'Safe Haven' for Creativity at Pixar." blogs.harvardbusiness.org, February 23, 2009.

———. "Pixar's Collective Genius." blogs.harvardbusiness.org, August 19, 2008.

Rao, Hayagreeva, Robert Sutton, and Allen P. Webb. "Innovation Lessons from Pixar: An Interview with Oscar-Winning Director Brad Bird." mckinseyquarterly.com, April 2008.

Rinehart, Carroll, Opening Minds through the Arts cofounder; opera with children expert, Tucson Unified School District. Interview by the author, April 2009.

Robinson, Peter. "Good Stuff: A Conversation with One of the Men Behind Pixar." nationalreview.com, December 23, 2004.

Romano, Lou, former Pixar employee. Personal communication, April 2009.

Rubin, Michael. *Droidmaker: George Lucas and the Digital Revolution.* Gainsville, FL: Triad Publishing Company, 2006.

Russell, Mike. "The Pixar Players." natoonline.org, May 2003.

Schlender, Brent. "Incredible: The Man Who Built Pixar's Innovation Machine." money.cnn.com/magazines/fortune, November 15, 2004.

———. "Pixar's Magic Man." money.cnn.com/magazines/fortune, May 17, 2006.

Schrage, Michael. *Serious Play: How the World's Best Companies Simulate to Innovate.* Boston, MA: Harvard Business School Press, 2000.

Sci Fi Wire. "John Ratzenberger, Pixar's Good Luck Charm, on *Up, Bugs* and *Toys 3.*" http://scifiwire.com, 2009.

Shankland, Stephen. "Schmidt: It's Google's Duty to Help Fix Ad Business." news.cnet.com, June 11, 2008.

Silverthorne, Sean. "Avoiding Tainted Love: How Pixar Builds Sustainable Creativity." blogsbnet.com, August 26, 2008.

Singer, Greg. "The Secret of Pixar Storytelling." awn.com, March 19, 2007.

Smith, Alvy Ray, Pixar cofounder. Interview by the author, April 2009.

Staff. "Disney/Pixar *Up*—Director, Producer, Interview." seenit.co.uk, April 22, 2009.

Taylor, William, and Polly LaBarre. "How Pixar Adds a New School of Thought to Disney." nytimes.com, January 29, 2006.

———. *Mavericks at Work: Why the Most Original Minds in Business Win.* New York: William Morrow, 2006.

Thompson, Kari, director of corporate communications, Target Corporation. Interview by the author, May 2009.

Vaughn, Harry. "Pixar Director Pete Docter Proves That *Up*
    Is Not Full of Hot Air." berkeleybeacon.com, April 30,
    2009.
Vesely, Jan, Opening Minds through the Arts cofounder; super-
    intendent of instruction and curriculum, Sunnyside
    School District. Interview by the author, April 2009.
Wamer, Rick, Opening Minds through the Arts program coor-
    dinator, Tucson Unified School District. Interview by
    the author, May 2009.
Warren, Chris. "Innovation Inc." americanwaymag.com,
    December 15, 2004.
Wickre, Karen, managing editor of the official Google Blog.
    Personal communication, April 2009.
Wloszczyna, Susan. "Pixar Moves on 'Up' with Its 10th Movie."
    http://usatoday.com, May 22, 2009.
Wood, Gaby. "John Lasseter: The Genius Shaping the Future of
    the Movies." observer.guardian.co.uk, January 18, 2009.
Wood, Jennifer M. "Creating the Pixar Phenomenon."
    moviemaker.com, February 3, 2007.
Wragg, Nate, Pixar employee. Personal communication, April
    2009.
Zimmer, George, founder and CEO, Men's Wearhouse. Inter-
    view by the author, August 2001.

To request Bill Capodagli for a Pixar Way or Disney Way
keynote presentation, please call 800-238-9958 or e-mail
dreamovations@aol.com.

Index

Alexin, Michael, 168–69
Allen, Tim, 177
Apple, 8, 26
Ashcraft, Joan, 59, 60
Attitude, 142
Ayers, Charlie, 155

Backstage processes, designing, 20–21
Barrie, J. M., 9
"Bead Factory" exercise, 117–18
Bedbury, Scott, 166
Ben Franklin Stores, 7–8
Bennis, Warren, 144
Bird, Brad, 19–20, 42, 45, 86
Black sheep, 19–20
Blanchard, Ken, 130
Brain trust, at Pixar, 42, 143–44
Bryan, Lowell L., 118
Bug's Life, A, 126–28, 130, 177
Bullies, 67–72
Business plans, quality and, 145

CalArts, 32
Carroll, Kevin, 165, 166
Cars, 177–78
Cast, recruiting, 18–20
Catalysts, for innovation, 52–53
Catmull, Ed, x–xii, 11, 14, 92, 118, 128–29, 132, 143, 144–45, 147, 148
    career of, 27–29
    catalysts for, 52
    culture of risk taking and, 60–61
    feedback and, 42–43
    organization building and, 27
    partnership with J. Lasseter, 34–35
    risk taking and, 77–78, 80
    talent scouting and, 44–45
    teamwork and, 41
Celebrations, 143
Chapman, Brenda, 42
Charmel, Patrick, 159–60

Childhood, remembering magic
    of, 1–4
Christensen, John, 93
Churchill, Sir Winston, 77
Collaboration, 51, 62
    inside, 140
    outside, 141
    at Pixar, 46
Commitment, 26
Continuing education, 53–54
Cool projects, working on,
    141–42
Corporate playgrounds, creat-
    ing, 137–47
Creative climates, 39–41
Creativity, 7–9
    at Pixar, 9–11
Creutz, Doug, 118, 121
Customer experiences, craft-
    ing, 17

Daniels, Phil, 143
Deming, W. Edwards, 10, 117
Disney, Roy, xi, 34
Disney, Walt, x, xi, 8, 34, 65, 72,
    139
    film sequels and, 14
    leadership of, 38
    training artists and, 54–55
Docter, Pete, 2, 42, 63, 68, 91, 97,
    126, 128

Dreamers, 144
Dreaming, 25–35, 78
DreamWorks, 71
Drucker, Peter, 43

Ewert, Doug, 162

Fagen, Elizabeth, 60
Failing forward, 77
Failures, 75–76
    celebrating, 78
    famous, 76–77
Feedback, delivering, at Pixar,
    42–43
Finding Nemo, 177
Forced fun time (FFT), 93–94
Ford, Henry, 7, 10, 76
Francis, Michael, 169
Fun, attitude and, 142

Gagné, Michel, 40
Geffen, David, 71
George Lucas Educational
    Foundation, 2
Goals, long-term, at Pixar, 45
Goethe, Johann Wolfgang von,
    148
Good, Craig, 137
Google, 8, 152–56
Gordon, Andrew, 176
Graham, Don, 54

Griffin Hospital, 156–60
Grisham, John, 76

Hansen, Ed, 32, 33
HP, 146
Hsieh, Tony, 170, 172, 173
Huizinga, Johan, 87

IBM, 145
Iger, Bob, 119
Improvisation, 138–39
Incredibles, The, 19–20, 177
Innovation
    actions for improving process
        of, 98–111
    catalysts for, 52–53
    play and, 87
    process metrics for, 122–23
Innovators, 144
International Play Association
    (IPA/USA), 83–84
Intrapreneurism, creating
    department of, 110

Jobs, Steve, x–xi, 88, 90–91, 118,
    125, 127
Johnson, Kelly, 78
Johnston, Ollie, 32
Jones, J. Eugene "Gene," 58–59,
    60
Jordan, Michael, 77

Kasner, Edward, 154
Katzenberg, Jeffery, 68–71
Koziak, Jodee, 169
Kresge's, 7
Krock, Ray, 7

Larson, Eric, 32
Lasseter, John, x–xii, 9, 11, 63, 68,
    118, 119–20, 126, 128, 131–32,
    168, 175, 176, 179
    career of, 30–34
    catalysts for, 52
    creative ideas and, 97
    details and, 17
    partnership with E. Catmull,
        34–35
Leadership
    creative, 146–47
    of Walt Disney, 38
Leadership values, of Pixar,
    118-119
Leek, Richard, 188–89
Lewis, Brad, 42
Lin, Alfred, 172–73
Luxo Jr., 175

McCarthy, Tom, 178–79
McColgin, Jerry, 138
McDonald's, 2
Men's Wearhouse, 160–63
Microsoft, 145

Miller, Ron, 33
Monsters, Inc., 177
Mr. Potato Head, 178
Murray, Bill, 176–78

Nelson, Randy, 14, 39, 55–56, 60,
    61–62, 63–64, 76, 138–40
    catalysts for, 52
Newell, Martin, 30
Newman, Randy, 177
Nike, 8, 163–66

Opening Minds Through the
    Arts (OMA), 2–3, 53, 56–60
    art and quotes of students of,
    182–91
Ortega, Kenny, 13
Overexposure, avoiding, 13–14
Overton, David, 98

Page, Larry, 155
Panaccione, Julie, 162, 163
Parker, Mark, 166
Patents, 146–47
Patton, George, 78
Peterson, Bob, 42
Pfeuffer, Roger, 59
Pixar, xi
    beginnings of, 25–35
    box-office results of, 120
    brain trust of, 42

collaborative spirit at, 46
commitment and, 26–27
continuing education at,
    53–56
creative climates at, 39–41
creativity at, 9–11
delivering feedback at, 42–43
fun facts about, 175–79
idea sharing at, 60
innovative process of, 122–23
leadership values of, 118–19
long-term goals and, 45
mutual respect and trust at,
    45–46
self-motivated personnel at,
    43–45
sequels at, 14–15
span of control at, 44
team proficiencies at, 61–62
teamwork at, 41–43
telling your story at, 15–16
unique playground of, 88–91
vision at, 38–39
Pixar University, 40, 53–56
Pixarians, 39, 41, 44–45
    teamwork and, 63
Planetree, 156, 157
Planning centers, 79
Play
    attitude and, 142
    benefits of, 84–85

importance of, 85–86

innovation and, 87

questions for, in organizations, 87–88

reasons for lack of, in companies, 86–87

seriousness of, 87

thinking, 91

Playgrounds, creating corporate,
   137–47

Plus-ing, 139–40

Poll, Donn, 3

Postmortems, 144–45

Powanda, Bill, 159

Proficiencies, team, at Pixar,
   61–62

Project Zero, 58

Prototypes, 78, 141

Quality, business plans and,
   145

Ramis, Harold, 161

Ranft, Joe, 68, 128

Ratatouille, 178

Ratzenberger, John, 176

Recess, 84–85

"Red Bead Factory" exercise,
   117–18

Respect, mutual, at Pixar, 45–46

Rich, Ben, 78

Rinehart, Carroll, 57, 60, 115

Risk taking, 77–78

   Catmull on, 80

   ideas to encourage, 78–80

Romano, Lou, 93

Rowling, J. K., 77

Rydstrom, Gary, 42

Schmidt, Eric, 156

Seidel, Steve, 58

Sequels, at Pixar, 14–15

Sets, building, 17–18

Shoup, Dick, 29

Sirotta, Milton, 154

Skinner, B. F., 178

Skunk works, 78–79

Slabin, Andrew, 14

Smith, Alvy Ray, x, 4, 44, 46, 71,
   92–93, 131

   career of, 27–30

Span of control, at Pixar, 44

Spielberg, Steven, 71

Stanton, Andrew, 42, 68, 70,
   128

Stapleton, Claire, 155

Station Agent, The, 178–79

Stories

   beginning with, 15–16

   importance of, 137

Storyboarding, 137–38

Sullivan, Louis, 52

Target, 166–69
Taylor, Frederick W., 10
Team proficiencies, at Pixar,
  61–62
Teamwork, at Pixar, 41–43
Thomas, Bob, 31
Thomas, Frank, 32
Thompson, Kari, 169
Toy Story, 2, 68–71, 125–26,
  176–77
Toy Story 2, 14–15, 126–31
Toy Story Midway Mania, 178
Training, 142
Transparency, 142–43
Trust, mutual, at Pixar, 45–46
Tucson University School
  District, 2, 53–54

Unkrich, Lee, 42, 90, 128

Van Gogh, Vincent, 77
Vesely, Jan, 60
Vision, at Pixar, 38–39

Wal-Mart, 8, 26
Wallis, Michael, 98
Walt Disney Company, The, xi,
  26

Walton, Sam, 8
Warner, Rick, 58, 64
WestEd, 57
White Castle, 7
Wieden, Dan, 166
Woolworth dime stores, 7
Workplaces, actions to fire up,
  88–94
  allowing personalized
    workspaces, 91–92
  allowing recognition by
    outsiders, 92–93
  creating unique playgrounds,
    88–91
  having mutual respect and
    trust, 93–94
  laughing at oneself, 94–95
  making time for celebrations,
    92
  think play!, 91
Wright, Frank Lloyd, 52
Wright, Orville, 77

Zappos, 170–73
Zimmer, George, 87, 161,
  162